The Japanese and Europe

The Japanese and Europe

Economic and Cultural Encounters

Marie Conte-Helm

ATHLONE
London & Atlantic Highlands, NJ

First published 1996 by
THE ATHLONE PRESS LTD
1 Park Drive, London NW11 7SG
and 165 First Avenue,
Atlantic Highlands, NJ 07716

British Library Cataloguing in Publication Data
*A catalogue record for this book is available
from the British Library*

ISBN 0 485 11461 5

Library of Congress Cataloging-in-Publication Data

Conte-Helm, Marie, 1949–
    The Japanese and Europe : economic and cultural
encounters / Marie Conte-Helm.
        p.   cm.
    Includes bibliographical references and index.
    ISBN 0-485-11461-5 (hardcover)
    1. Europe--Relations--Japan.   2. Japan--Relations-
-Europe.
I. Title.
D1065.J3C66   1996
303.48'25204--dc20   95-23893
                                                                    CIP

Typeset by
Bibloset

Printed and bound in Great Britain by
the University Press, Cambridge

In Memory of My Mother and Father

CONTENTS

Acknowledgements

In exploring the experience of the Japanese in Europe, interviews have been essential to my research. Particular thanks are therefore due to the Daiwa Anglo-Japanese Foundation who funded my research travel in Europe and to Christopher Everett, its Director-General, for his kind support.

Establishing contacts and arranging appointments was a mammoth task and, for this, I most heartily thank Kobayashi Masao and Kurita Nobufumi of the Japan External Trade Organization (JETRO) in London for their considerable help. JETRO's European offices proved an invaluable source of advice and assistance during my travels. Thanks are due to the following JETRO people, some of whom have since moved on: Kobayashi Takao and Haruhiko Okada in Paris, Nakamura Toshihiko and Maeda Shigeki in Düsseldorf, Nagasaka Toshihisa in Amsterdam, Iwai Yoshiyuki in Brussels, and Nureki Taiji and Hikota Yoshiro in Madrid.

I would like to express my gratitude to Minister Kitabatake Tamon, formerly at the Embassy of Japan, London, for his advice and support and to Ohmori Fujio who provided useful data on the education of Japanese children overseas and arranged visits to Monbusho and Oizumi High School in Tokyo. I am similarly grateful to staff at the Embassies of Japan in Paris, Brussels, the Hague and Madrid and to the Japanese Consul in Barcelona.

Visits to several Japanese schools in Europe furnished valuable insights into the Japanese overseas education system and the 'returnee problem'. For access to and tours around their schools, I wish to thank Professor Muta Yasuaki of the Institut Culturel Franco Japonais at Montigny-le-Bretonneux, Matsuda Toshifumi, Principal of the Japanische Internationale

Schüle in Düsseldorf, and Matsumoto Kuniyoshi and Nakayama Hiroyuki of the Japanese School of Brussels.

I have met and talked with so many individuals in carrying out this project that it is difficult to mention them all. Among those who gave generously of their time to discuss various dimensions of the Japanese and Europe with me, I would like to thank the following:

In France, Abe Yoshio of the Japanese Chamber of Commerce and Industry (JCCI), Kawahara Tatsu of Mitsui & Co., Hasegawa Michio of Saint-Germain France, Nagasawa Yoshitaka of Price Waterhouse, Koito Junji of the Association Amicale des Ressortissants en France, Graham Lord of the Office Franco-Japonais d'Études Économique and Philippe Parfait of DATAR's Invest in France Agency who, while based in London, provided useful background on the Japanese in France.

In Germany, Miyai Junji of the JCCI, Hagiwara Atsushi of Nissan Deutschland, Yokonishi Keiso of Shionogi & Co and Wolfgang Jansen of the Nordrhein-Westfalen (NRW) Economic Development Corporation.

In the Netherlands, Maiya Masahiko of the Hotel Okura, Toos van Leeuven of Canon Europe, Inoue Toshihiro and Kimoto Kiyomi of Nagasaki Holland Village Nederland, Mark Smallegange of the Netherlands Foreign Trade Agency, A.G. Karl of the Dutch and Japanese Trade Federation, Mirjam Schuit and Martin Dorsman of the Netherlands Foreign Investment Agency, Mrs Osada of the JCCI and for liaison support, Richard Burke and Corrie Siahaya-Van Nierop of the Canon Foundation.

In Belgium, Sato Masahiko and Miyasaka Yasuo of Nihonjinkai, Takahashi Tatsuo and Miyadai Harayuki of Toyota Motor Europe, Fabienne Fuji L'Hoost of the Belgium-Japan Association and Chamber of Commerce and, for background information and statistics, John Richardson of the European Commmission's Unit for EC/Japan Relations. I wish to thank particularly Harashima Masae of Price Waterhouse, Brussels, for his candid observations and help with contacts elsewhere in Europe.

In Spain, Jaime Montalvo Dominguez de La Torre of the Ministry of Commerce and Tourism and Danbara Akihisa of Price Waterhouse Madrid, Nemoto Eri of CIDEM and Saeki Takahashi of Price Waterhouse, Barcelona. Again, my particular thanks to Hirano Hideaki of Nissan Motor Iberica whose consecutive experiences of North East England, the Netherlands and Spain have illustrated the growing cultural adaptability of the Japanese.

It is almost impossible to acknowledge adequately the help and support

I have received from the Anglo-Japanese community in the UK. London-based bodies such as the Embassy of Japan, Japan Foundation and Anglo-Japanese Economic Institute have supplied factual data and photographic material. Beyond London, Japanese companies and individuals in the regions have provided much of the impetus for this book by the successful working partnerships they have achieved. My thanks to Yasutaka Junichi of Nippon Seiko Kaisha (NSK) whose many years spent in the UK gave him the opportunity to view Europe and Japan from a point somewhere in between. I am grateful for his advice and comments on Chapter 3.

For permission to reproduce photographs and other materials, my thanks to Tim Macmillan, Iain Lanyon, In-Print Publishing, the Victoria & Albert Museum, British Nuclear Fuels, the British Tourist Authority, the Japan Information and Cultural Centre, the Daiwa Anglo-Japanese Foundation and Monbusho.

For Chapter 5 and perspectives on the Japanese in Europe, the Japan Festival 1991 was a wonderful inspiration in establishing, through so many of its events, a common ground. To Japanese and British friends who shared in the experience, I look back fondly on a very special time.

Finally, a special thank you to my husband, Bill, who has generously advised, cajoled and comforted throughout the writing of this book and to my daughter, Jessica, who has helped to keep me cheerful in all its stages.

Note on Order of Japanese Names

Japanese names are presented in the usual order of surname first and given name second throughout the text.

Introduction

The great wave of Japanese investment in Europe in the 1980s and early 90s has been much analysed in its economic impact and its implications for comparative management styles. Yet, with the establishment of Japanese production bases and other operations in Europe has come an influx of Japanese company personnel and their families who have added a further layer to complex multicultural European societies, while retaining a distinct identity in their midst.

The Japanese and Europe is the subject of this book, but it sets out to explore, within it, a number of themes. The present-day Japanese presence in Europe and the everyday grappling with long-held images and stereotypes in our mutual encounters can be viewed in the context of first meetings and historic ties. Japan's relationship with Europe has a distant past as well as a more recent history in the trade frictions of the 1970s and 80s and the investments made in Europe in the lead-up to 1992.

The formation of the Single European Market has brought the Japanese in large numbers into the United Kingdom, France, Germany, Spain, the Netherlands and Belgium. These are the countries which are the focus of this study, though other European countries which have attracted important investment from Japan, such as Ireland, Italy, Austria and Portugal, might similarly have been included.

Such a selective focus has been borne of the necessity to scale down a subject which is essentially enormous in scope. The choice of countries is also tied to the aim of this book which is to provide a broad overview of the Japanese experience of Europe and the issues and circumstances which are faced in leaving Japan.

The overview approach inevitably runs the risk of generalization and I hope that, in incorporating findings based on interviews throughout, I have been able to tie down some assertions while qualifying others. No society is static, and a rapidly changing Japan may well leave the highly travelled and internationally experienced Japanese manager asking of Chapter 3: 'But where do I fit in?'. I hope that I have allowed for different views and experiences while, in the end, opting for the general picture.

In attempting to provide a feel for how the Japanese live in Europe, I have been equally preoccupied with the theme of how the Japanese view Europe, past and present. Coming to terms with the unwieldy geographical mass that is Europe and the bureacratic entity of the European Community (EC) has long challenged Japanese perceptions of national differences and regional cultures. Images and expectations are thus set against the realities of a posting to a particular place at a particular time and what that has meant for company employees and families alike.

The Japanese presence in Europe is gradually having an impact too upon the European view and awareness of Japan. If the 1980s have witnessed what some would term an 'economic assault' on Europe, so has the Japanese culture and way of life become more familiar and accessible as a result of investment from Japan. The charting of images must allow for this two-way traffic in adjusting perspectives, and a learning curve that affects both East and West.

This book is aimed at the Japanese as well as the western reader. On one level, its description of Japanese facilities – from shops to restaurants to social clubs and schools – may offer a 'survival guide' to Japan in Europe. The 'listing' is by no means comprehensive, however, but is featured in an attempt to convey aspects of the Japanese lifestyle abroad that arise from how the Japanese live in Japan. The issues of social integration and adaptation are complex ones and can only be approached from the perspective of the nature of Japanese society itself.

In the realm of images, it is frequently observed that the Japanese in Europe – both residents and tourists – are prone to being photographed in groups. The group photograph does relay something of the Japanese collective consciousness and the tendency to stick together both at home and abroad. What it cannot relay, however, is anything of the individuals which it portrays. The image of the Japanese in Europe will ultimately be set against the reality of those individuals who have moved beyond the Japanese frame and made their presence felt.

1   Japan and Europe: Perspectives from the Past

Remembering first encounters is the prerogative of the romantic and the historian. Japan's long relationship with Europe has been amply treated by both. It was, however, trade that brought Japan and Europe into the same orbit in the sixteenth century and it was Japan's reopening to trade that established the subsequent pattern of bilateral ties. Today, global economic forces dominate where once the expansionist ambitions of individual colonialist powers held sway. The social and cultural consequences of this intercourse between Japan and Europe and the mutual images that have evolved form part of the history of commercial exchange.

The first Europeans to arrive in Japan were three Portuguese traders who landed on the island of Tanegashima off the coast of southern Kyushu when the Chinese junk on which they were bound for Macau sailed off course in a typhoon. The year was 1543 and the event, unmomentous in itself, was to open the first phase in the history of Japan's links with Europe.

The arrival of Portuguese merchant ships in Kyushu a year or two after this episode in accidental tourism was a more deliberate attempt on the part of the East Indies trade establishment to extend their sphere of influence into this new-found land. The first ships and their wares excited great interest amongst the native Japanese population. A new word, *tanegashima*, crept into the language to describe the imported European muskets which were soon being copied in Japan.[1] The Portuguese trade was swiftly deemed to be of mutual benefit and duly received the sanction of Kyushu's most powerful feudal lords or *daimyo* as they were known.

Inextricably bound up with this trade was missionary activity. Indeed, the Japanese noted the respect with which the Portuguese merchants treated their missionary passengers aboard the first trading ships and proved receptive to the message which they relayed. Acknowledgement of the potential for Christian converts in Japan came with the arrival of the Portuguese Jesuit missionary, Francis Xavier, at Kagoshima in August 1549. Supported in their early efforts by the lord of Satsuma, Francis Xavier and his compatriots first preached Christianity in Japan.

Japanese official tolerance of Christian proselytizing has been partly attributed to the close association between the Jesuits and traders and the desire on the part of various *daimyo* to profit from foreign trade.[2] Just how much of the Christian message was in fact understood, given the limited command of Japanese of the Jesuits and the scarcity of interpreters, is debatable.

If a mixture of curiosity and self-interest informed the early Japanese reaction to the Portuguese, they, on their part, can be seen to have responded with unqualified enthusiasm to their new eastern trading partners and brethren. Francis Xavier described the Japanese as 'the best people so far discovered and it seems to me that among unbelievers no people can be found to excel them'.[3] He is said to have remarked upon their good manners, sense of honour, propriety and duty[4] and, despite difficulties experienced during his two-year stay, came to judge Japan as 'a rich and fertile field from whence copious and joyful results may be expected'.[5]

By the time of his return to Goa in 1552, Xavier could claim a number of Christian converts in Japan and, with his support, the size of the Jesuit mission there gradually increased. When a review of mission activity in Japan was undertaken by the Visitor Alessandro Valignano in 1582, it was calculated that there were 150,000 Christians (mainly concentrated in western Japan) and 200 churches, with no more than twenty fathers administering to the needs of the faithful.[6] Jesuit seminaries in Nagasaki and elsewhere had become centres for the copying of European votive images and, in this way too, the message of Christianity was spread to the widest possible following. The arrival of a printing press in 1590 enabled the Jesuits to provide instruction in European engraving techniques and greatly facilitated this process.[7]

There was, to be sure, an element of fashionable curiosity in the ready adoption of Christianity and aspects of western dress by some Japanese followers. The carrying of rosaries and other such Christian accoutrements signalled a worldliness and subscription to foreign taste at a time when Japan's insularity from the West remained otherwise intact. Indeed a letter written by the missionary, Francisco Pasio, in September 1594 suggests that such practices were not only confined to believers:

The same is true even of those *daimyo* who are not Christian. They wear rosaries of driftwood on their breasts, hang a crucifix from the shoulder or waist, and sometimes even hold a handkerchief. Some, who are especially kindly disposed, have memorized the Our Father and Hail Mary, and recite them as they walk in the streets. This is not done in ridicule of the Christians, but simply to show off their familiarity with the latest fashion, or because they think it good and effective in bringing success in daily life. This has led them to spend no small sums in ordering oval earrings bearing the likeness of Our Lord and Holy Mother.[8]

Namban screen paintings of this period reflect the interest with which Europeans were regarded. The word *namban*, literally 'southern barbarian'. refers both to the trade route via which Portuguese vessels made their way to the East and to the nature of the passengers whose otherness was thus defined. Such paintings offer up fascinating observations of the appearance and manners of the Portuguese merchants and missionaries as well as the converts who emulated their foreign style.

While the Japanese view of Europe during these years was primarily determined by the imported culture of the Portuguese, more direct experience was gained by the first official mission to Europe consisting of four youthful Japanese emissaries from Kyushu who left their home fiefdoms in 1582 and returned some eight years later in 1590. Arranged by the Visitor Valignano with an eye towards consolidating the Jesuit position in Japan, all aspects of the mission were designed to impress. Valignano's motives in this respect were clearly set out:

In sending the boys to Portugal and Rome our intention is two-fold. Firstly it is to seek the help, both temporal and spiritual which we need in Japan. Secondly it is to make the Japanese aware of the glory and greatness of Christianity, and of the majesty of the princes and lords who profess it, and of the greatness and wealth of our kingdoms and cities, and of the honour in which our religion is held and the power it possesses in them. These Japanese boys will be witnesses who will have seen these things, and being persons of such quality they will be able to return to Japan and to say what they have seen.[9]

The official party landed at Lisbon in August 1584 and travelled on to Madrid where they were lavishly hosted by Philip II, the powerful monarch of Spain and Portugal. Likened by some to the Magi,[10] the 'wise men from the East' proceeded on their pilgrimage to Italy and, after visiting Florence, were transported to Rome to be received by Pope

Japanese *Namban* screen painting depicting the Portuguese in Japan, 1600
(courtesy of the Board of Trustees of the Victoria & Albert Museum).

Gregory XIII. Their procession on horseback through the centre of the
city in full Japanese dress, complete with samurai swords, was surrounded
by pomp and ceremony. A 300-gun salute from the Castel Sant'Angelo
marked their arrival and huge crowds waited to greet them at St Peter's
Square.[11]

An important consequence of this 20-month-long triumphal tour of
Portugal, Spain and Italy was a papal bull recognizing the exclusive rights
of the Jesuits to continue their missionary work in Japan. On another
level, however, the Japanese mission which took in some seventy different
towns and cities across three countries succeeded in generating the first real
awareness of Japan in Europe.

The records and memorabilia of the 1582 mission convey something of
the curiosity and enthusiasm with which the visitors were received and
with which they responded to their hosts and surroundings.[12] At the village
of Evora in Portugal, the Japanese youths were welcomed with a high
mass in the Cathedral conducted by the Archbishop, Dom Theotonio de
Braganza. They were later entertained at a banquet and showered with
gifts. The Archbishop's sister-in-law, Dona Catherina, was so fascinated
by their dress that she had a Japanese costume made for her own son and
contemplated the introduction of kimono as an exotic addition to the more
usual Portuguese festival wear.

Wherever they went, the envoys were continually on display, and not
only their dress but their eating habits and general demeanour were much
commented upon. By the end of the century, over seventy publications,
in a number of different languages, had recorded the details of the mission
and particularly their reception in Rome. While not the very first Japanese

visitors to Europe (Francis Xavier had sent the young Japanese convert, christened Bernard, to Portugal, Spain and Italy in 1552), the 1582 mission was to exert the greater impact in cultural terms, while politically, for the Jesuits, it was considered an unqualified success.

Ironically, despite the papal sanction of Jesuit rights in Japan, the last decade of the sixteenth century saw Jesuit activity and the course of Christianity undermined by both internal and external forces. In 1587, the military ruler, Hideyoshi Toyotomi (1536–1598), took the Christian community by surprise when, without warning, he issued an edict prohibiting Christian activity in Japan. While not strictly enforced, it marked a change in a climate that was made more turbulent by the arrival from Manila in 1593 of Spanish Franciscan, Dominican and Augustinian friars. Conflict between the different religious orders and national rivalries exacerbated an increasingly tense situation as a succession of shoguns and feudal lords began to question the increasing sphere of foreign influence in Japan.

Isolated incidents of persecution and martyrdom of Christians followed as further anti-Christian orders were issued by the Shogun, Tokugawa Ieyasu (1541–1616), between 1611 and 1614. When Ieyasu was succeeded by Hidetada (1616–1622), the persecution of Christians was intensified and Christianity was suppressed or driven underground. It has been estimated that over 3,000 Christians were directly martyred in Japan between 1597 and 1660 and one source sets Christian casualties as high as 200,000 for this period.[13]

These same years saw the arrival of other Europeans in Japan as Dutch and English merchant ships began to challenge the Portuguese monopoly of trade with the East. In 1600 the Englishman William Adams (1564–1620), pilot of the Dutch ship *Liefde*, was shipwrecked with other surviving crew members off the coast of Ito. Adams was born in Gillingham, Kent, and has been immortalized as the first Englishman to set foot on Japanese soil. As so many biographical and fictional narratives relate, he went on to become adviser to the Shogun, Tokugawa Ieyasu, and lived out the rest of his days in Japan. His body was laid to rest at Yokosuka, the Japanese port town which has in recent years been twinned with Adams's birthplace in Kent.

The relationship between Adams and Ieyasu was of some importance to the future of the European trade with Japan, for Adams provided another perspective on contemporary power politics and religious conflict in Europe as well as advising the Shogun on navigational matters. As the Dutch and the English consolidated their trading positions with Japan in 1609 and 1613 respectively, he was employed as a diplomatic agent and even directed the construction of a European-style ship for the Shogun.[14] His loyalties were rewarded when he was made a samurai by Ieyasu and endowed with a large estate.

Rivalries and in-fighting between the Portuguese and the Spanish soon enveloped the Dutch and English merchant communities in Japan. Growing suspicions of the broader agenda of Christian missionaries intensified and inevitably rebounded on the Christians themselves as well as the future prospects for European trade with Japan.

The culmination of these events was the enactment of a series of edicts in 1633, 1635 and 1639 which effectively closed the country to outside influence for more than two centuries. The Spaniards had been banished from Japan in 1624. Now, all Portuguese Jesuit missionaries were expelled from the country, and trade with Portugal was banned. The Japanese were prohibited from travelling abroad and from building large sea-going vessels. The penalties for contravention of these measures was death for those who dared to return.

Lack of profitability and other problems had led the English to close their trading post in Japan in 1623. When the English attempted to reactivate earlier trading links in 1673, the Japanese resolutely spurned an initial overture on the grounds that Charles II was married to Catherine of Braganza, the daughter of the King of Portugal.[15]

Only the Dutch, whose presence in Japan was untainted by Christian missionary activity were able through these years of virtual isolation to maintain a foothold there. From 1641, Deshima, an artificial island off the coast of Nagasaki, served as their self-contained and carefully monitored trading base in Japan. Their numbers were small and the Dutch residents of Deshima were forbidden to travel within Japan or to fraternize beyond the confines of their island 'prison' with the Japanese.

The director of the Dutch factory and his limited entourage were allowed an annual audience with the Shogun in Edo (present-day Tokyo), essentially an opportunity to bestow tributes and to report to and reassure the supreme ruler of Japan that their servile status remained undiminished. The German physician Engelbert Kaempfer (1651–1716), who served the Dutch settlement between 1690 and 1692, recorded details of the embassies made to Edo during this period. Referring to the Shogun as the 'Emperor', he described the indignities which the Dutch were forced to endure for the sake of trade:

> he ordered us to take off our Capper, or Cloak, being our Garment of Ceremony, then to stand upright, that he might have a full view of us; again to walk, to stand still, to compliment each other, to dance, to jump, to play the drunkard, to speak broken

Japanese painting of the Dutch settlement at Nagasaki, early seventeenth century (Victoria & Albert Museum).

Japanese, to read Dutch, to paint, to sing, to put our cloaks on and off. Mean while we obey'd the Emperor's commands in the best manner we could, I joined to my dance a love-song in high German. In this manner, and with innumerable such other apish tricks, we must suffer ourselves to contribute to the Emperor's and the Court's diversion.[16]

Communication between the Japanese and the Dutch was initially in Portuguese but, by the second half of the seventeenth century, there were interpreters in Nagasaki who could both speak and read Dutch and who developed deeper interests as a result.[17]

Anti-Christian feeling had led to an import ban on western books in 1630. Any knowledge of European scientific advances was thus denied to the Japanese until the narrow channel of access to Dutch learning was gradually widened. The restrictions on imported western books, including those in Chinese translation, were eased in 1720. Then, in 1740, the ruling Shogun, Yoshimune (1716–1745), ordered two scholars, Noro Genjo and Aoki Konyo, to embark upon Dutch studies. This resulted in the compilation of Noro's *Japanese Explanations of Dutch Botany* (*Oranda Honso Wage*) in 1750 and Aoki's dictionary of the Dutch language in 1758. The greater significance of these scholastic efforts was that, through the encouragement of the Shogun, the respectability of Dutch studies was extended beyond Nagasaki to the whole of Japan.[18]

The name accorded to Dutch studies by the Japanese was *rangaku* or *komo bunka*, 'red-hair learning', signifying the lighter colouring of the Europeans with perhaps some demonic connotations derived from

Buddhist painted images. One Japanese visitor to a Dutch ship somewhat overstated this stereotype:

> When we went aboard, the captain and many others took off
> their hats to salute us. They have dark, sallow faces, yellow hair,
> and green eyes. They seem to appear from nowhere, and are
> just like goblins and demons. Who would not run away from
> them in fright.[19]

Despite such xenophobic outpourings about the Dutch, Japan was provided with a window to Europe through the long years of isolation from the West. Following the relaxation of censorship, scientific books and treatises written in Dutch were imported into Japan through the settlement at Deshima. Translations of a wide variety of texts were methodically produced by the growing number of Japanese Dutch specialists who gravitated to Nagasaki. Feudal lords, anxious to learn something of western advances, sent retainers to Nagasaki for the express purpose of vicarious foreign study. The phrase *rampeki* or 'the Dutch craze' came into common use and reflected a growing curiosity and taste for the exotic which was for a time embodied in all things Dutch.[20]

There were complex reactions to some aspects of western learning in Japan. The Shinto scholar, Hirata Atsutane (1776–1843), was sceptical, for example, of scientific theories which put the sun – so central to Japanese mythology – into astronomical perspective:

> The reasons those barbarians spew forth such shallow false-
> hoods . . . is because they were born in filthy, remote countries,
> far from the Divine Land, and have had no opportunity to
> hear the ancient words from the divine mouth of Musubi
> no kami.[21]

On the other hand, Hirata openly acknowledged the importance of those European scientific advances which did not clash with his Shinto beliefs:

> It goes without saying how accomplished they are in astronomy
> and geography; people have also been amazed by the precision
> of their machines. They are particularly skilled in medicine and
> the preparation of drugs. It has doubtless been the will of the
> gods that European medical books have been brought here in
> ever-increasing numbers and have attracted wide attention.[22]

Playing a crucial role in the dissemination of medical and scientific achievements in Europe were the various physicians who served at the Dutch settlement at Deshima. Englebert Kaempfer, the German doctor who was in Japan from 1690 to 1692, has already been referred to. His extensive notes and observations on Japan were consolidated in his *History of Japan* (1729) which was published after his

Utagawa Toyoharu, 'A Perspective View of French Churches in Holland', woodblock print based on views of the Forum in Rome, 1780–1800 (Victoria & Albert Museum).

death and helped to redirect the flow of knowledge from Japan to Europe.

Philipp Franz von Siebold (1790–1866), another German physician of note, visited Japan over two periods in his career. Between 1823 and 1830 he served the medical needs of the Dutch at Deshima. Decades later, in 1859, he returned to Japan to pursue his researches and to promote Dutch–Japanese relations until his departure in 1862. Von Siebold published the results of his early studies of Japan and the Japanese in a major work, *Nippon. Archiv Zür Bescheibung von Japan* (1832–1854). His extensive collections of ethnological, natural scientific and other materials related to Japan formed the core of the Museum of Ethnology in Leiden and have been a valuable source of study for subsequent generations of Japan scholars.

For their part, the Japanese of this period collected all manner of European curiosities imported via the Dutch, from watches to scientific instruments to views of European cities. The latter were copied as another export, the technique of copperplate etching, brought contemporary European subject matter and the art of linear perspective into Japan. European painting manuals made an impact upon such Japanese artists of the day as Kokan Shiba (1738–1818) who applied the new principles to the depiction of Mount Fuji and other Japanese themes. Meanwhile, a different blend of art and science was achieved by the painter and print

Utagawa Yoshitora, 'Imagined View of the Port of London', woodblock print, 1856 (Victoria & Albert Museum).

designer, Okyo Maruyama (1733–1795) whose fascination with western perspective and illusionism was fuelled by observing and copying European peep-shows.

One can point to various legacies from the Portuguese phase of contact with Japan. In the so-called 'Christian Century', many Portuguese loan-words crept into the Japanese language for commodities that had been hitherto unknown. *Hankuchi* (for handkerchief), *pan* (for bread) and even *tempura* (for the deep-fried culinary contribution of the Portuguese to Japanese cuisine) are still in use today. Christianity itself, all but stifled in the early years of the seventeenth century, surprisingly endured through the secret observances of some members of the Nagasaki faithful during the long years of the repressive Tokugawa regime. One author has isolated the musket and tobacco as the only permanent contributions of the Portuguese[23] but the tenor of Japan's early relations with and views of the West was clearly established by the presence of their missionaries and traders in the country.

The legacy of the Dutch in Japan is more complex. Confined to Deshima as they were, the Dutch traders could hardly be viewed as evangelists actively preaching the gospel of European enlightenment. Rather, they were content to have a small but exclusive slice of the trade with Japan when only a slice was on offer. To maintain this precarious privilege, they accepted the restrictions placed upon them by the Japanese authorities. As anti-foreign paranoia eventually reached a state of equilibrium, however, Nagasaki and the Dutch settlement at Deshima began to exert a gravitational pull on those forces in Japan with a thirst for outside knowledge. Dutch studies provided at first a niggling and eventually a much more profound awareness that a world existed outside Japan and that it was a world the Japanese could not afford to ignore.

There were periodic attempts by other western powers to establish contact with Japan during the years of seclusion. Russian, British and American vessels increasingly appeared in Japanese waters seeking access to a harbour for supplies. Colonial expansion and maritime necessity meant that Japan, by the middle of the nineteenth century, had come into the sphere of European and American interests in the East. By 1853, those interests could no longer be kept at bay and the Japanese were essentially presented with an offer they could not refuse.

The arrival of Commodore Matthew Perry and his squadron of ships at Uraga Harbour on 8 July 1853 brought an impressive show of western naval power into direct and meaningful juxtaposition with the request from the American President, Millard Fillmore, to an opening of trade relations with Japan. Pressure was intensified with the arrival of the Russian Admiral Putiatin and his fleet in Nagasaki in August of that same year. Perry returned in February 1854 for his answer and, faced with the awesome and convincing evidence of the superior military strength of the West, the Japanese shogunate conceded to demands to trade.

The consequence of Perry's prising open of Japan to the West in 1854 was the subsequent signing of commercial treaties between Japan, the United States and the major European powers by 1858. These treaties included a 'most favoured nation' clause extending privileges accorded to one trading partner to all others. They further provided for the opening of particular ports to foreigners (initially Nagasaki, Hakodate, and Kanagawa – though Yokohama replaced the latter – and later Kobe, Osaka, Niigata and Edo). The terms of the treaties additionally allowed for the imposition of a very low rate of tariff for foreign goods coming into Japan, and the exemption of foreigners from the jurisdiction of Japanese courts. The latter particularly rankled as such rights did not apply to the Japanese abroad. The so-called 'unequal treaties' came to be viewed as a galling symbol of Japan's unequal relationship with the West. Their revision took place in 1894 and enactment of the revision only in 1899. In the intervening years of political and social change, Japan devoted herself wholeheartedly to the process of catching up with the West.

This process incorporated many phases including first the arrival of European and American diplomats and traders in Japan followed by the *yatoi* or 'government foreign employees' who helped to transform the country from a feudal isolationist kingdom into a modern industrial state. The first decade following the reopening of Japan was rife with internal

Utagawa Sadahide, An Englishman and a Chinese from Nanking in Yokohama, 1861 (Victoria & Albert Museum).

conflict as reactionary forces resisted the circumstances imposed upon Japan under western pressure. A weakened Tokugawa Shogunate was eventually brought down in the power struggle that followed and, in 1868, with the restoration of the Emperor to power, the Meiji era (1868–1912), Japan's 'age of enlightenment' was begun.

The slogan 'western technology, Japanese values' suitably summed up the ethos of Meiji Japan for, in the monumental effort to catch up with the West, the practice of taking the best from both worlds prevailed. Japan's European trading partners played a central role in the areas of foreign diplomacy and technological assistance in those early days of renewed contact, with the British and the French vying for supremacy in the race to gain influence with the new government. British support for the pro-imperial forces and French backing of the *Bakufu* (government of the Shogun) in the civil war of 1868 helped to determine their relative positions in the new order.

Britain contributed comprehensively to the modernization of Japan in the second half of the nineteenth century and to the international diplomatic efforts that later equalized her status. The first British Minister in Japan from 1859 to 1864, Sir Rutherford Alcock, saw British trading interests rise to pre-eminence in difficult times while his successor from 1865 to 1882, Sir Harry Parkes, exerted efforts to ensure that British technology and expertise were employed in the reshaping of Japan.[24]

After 1868 Japan embarked upon a programme of organizational and infrastructural change that affected virtually all aspects of economic, political and social life. Dutch studies and technical support were displaced by other foreign influences. Britain took the lead in naval matters, the Royal Navy providing the model for the Imperial Japanese Navy. France and later Germany served as the sources for Japan's modern army as well as her system of primary school education. The police and judicial systems were French-inspired, while Germany dominated in the field of medical training. For a central banking system, Japan looked to Belgium.

Government foreign employees or *yatoi* came in large numbers to Japan with Britain, France, the United States and Germany supplying the greater proportion of these so-called 'live machines'. Of the more than 3,000 *yatoi* who worked in Japan during the Meiji period, nearly half were British.[25] The British dominated the Public Works Ministry and were responsible for the building of Japan's railways, telegraph, lighthouses and harbours as well as the postal system.

Not surprisingly, links formed in the early days following Japan's reopening produced what has been termed a 'contagion effect'[26] whereby networks of personal contacts and language skills developed in one organizational framework were extended to other fields. This applied to the French who had established a foothold in Yokohama with the building of iron mills there from 1866. French influence in Japanese military affairs similarly drew on the earlier relationship forged by the French military mission to the shogunate and the founding of the French language school in Yokohama in 1865. Later, when Japan looked to German models for her constitution and army, a more widespread German influence on governmental organizational systems resulted.

Foreign instructors were employed in a number of technical fields in the Imperial College of Engineering. Here again, Britain dominated with Henry Dyer (1848–1918), a graduate of Glasgow University, appointed as its first principal in 1873. In 1877, the architect Josiah Conder (1852–1920), another Briton, joined the college as Professor of Architecture.

Conder was one of many westerners who contributed to the changing face of Japan during the Meiji period, both through his own work and that of the Japanese students whom he trained. His projects were diverse and eclectic, including the design of some seventy European-style buildings in brick and stone materials. Of these, the *Rokumeikan* or 'deer-cry pavilion', a state-owned guesthouse and social club, achieved the greatest notoriety, for it came to symbolize Japan's aspirations to attain equal status in the eyes of the West. The building was completed in 1883 to a Renaissance-style design and its interior decor strove to emulate the ballrooms, music rooms, games rooms and parlours of the Victorian world.

Modernization and westernization were interchangeable forces in Meiji Japan. Even the architects of Japan's reform were not immune to the excesses that followed the vogue for European fashions as the following account suggests:

> The most notorious affair was a fancy-dress ball (*fuanshi boru*), held at the official residence of Prime Minister Ito on April 20, 1887. The four hundred guests were greeted by the host, dressed as a Venetian nobleman, and the hostess, in a Spanish gown of yellow silk and wearing a mantilla. Miss Ito was dressed as an Italian peasant girl. Prince Arisugawa came as a European knight and Prince Kitashirakawa in the scarlet robes of a Southern European nobleman.[27]

Ito Hirobumi and his fellow-players in this spectacle were indulging, it would seem, in Japan's equivalent of *japonaiserie* – the contemporary European fascination with a fancy-dress image of Japan.

The Japanese image of Europe in the second half of the nineteenth century was the product of a multitude of sources. For many, Europe was embodied in the foreign presence in Japan and the changing styles of architecture, dress and musical taste that were being absorbed. The impact of European culture was apparent in the settings of the *Rokumeikan*, but more significantly in developments in the Japanese art world which increasingly looked to Europe for inspiration. For a time, 'Meiji western painting' all but displaced Japan's traditional painting techniques with indigenous versions of French Impressionist and Post-Impressionist art.

One must look beyond Japan, however, to uncover the primary sources for the Japanese image of Europe in this period. These may be found in the cumulative experience of so many Japanese students or emissaries who embarked upon the 'grand tour' in the late *Bakufu* and early Meiji periods through official or private means.

A Japanese *Bakufu* mission first made its way to Europe in 1862 with the primary goal of persuading the European treaty powers to postpone the opening of further treaty ports in Japan. Unrest in the foreign settlements following the opening of Japan made such a postponement desirable and, as a result of this mission, Britain, Russia, France and Holland reached agreement with the Japanese.

The months spent in Europe by the official party of some forty men provided an opportunity to experience and evaluate the diverse lifestyles and customs of Japan's European trading partners. The interpreter, Fukuzawa Yukichi, later wrote[28] of their culture shock and wonder as questions of etiquette, communication and taste arose. They arrived in Paris, heavily laden with dozens of large oil lamps and hundreds of cases of polished rice, certain that 'agreeable food would not be available in foreign lands'. Despite concerns as to whether a single hotel could be found to accommodate the whole party, the 600-room Hotel du Louvre proved so spacious that 'our real anxiety became the possibility of losing our way in the maze of halls and corridors'.

The Japanese curiosity about all facets of European life spilled over into Fukuzawa's account:

> when I saw a hospital, I wanted to know how it was run – who paid the running expenses; when I visited a bank, I wished to learn how the money was deposited and paid out. By similar first hand queries, I learned something of the postal system and the military conscription then in force in France but not in England . . . In some of the more complicated matters I might achieve an understanding five or ten days after they were explained to me. But all in all, I learned much from this initial tour of Europe.

The *Bakufu* party travelled from France to England, from Holland to Germany and then on to Russia. Frequently journeying by train – another new experience – their itinerary took in:

> the headquarters and buildings of the naval and military posts, factories, both governmental and private, banks, business offices, religious edifices, educational institutions, club houses, hospitals – including even the actual performances of surgical operations.

By way of recreation, Fukuzawa recalled: 'We were often invited to dinners in the homes of important personages, and to dancing parties; we were treated to a continual hospitality until at times we returned exhausted to our lodgings.'

Referring to Japan's 'special relationship' with Holland and the fact that some of the mission members spoke Dutch, Fukuzawa wrote of Holland as 'our second homeland' and 'the country in Europe which gave us the kindest welcome'.

Not so full an account exists of the impressions of other Japanese visitors to Europe in the pre-Meiji period. In 1863, Ito Hirobumi, along with four other Choshu clansmen, secretly left Japan to see Europe and to study for a short period at University College, London. The 'Choshu Five', as they have become known, went on to prominent leadership roles in the

Japanese students of Satsuma clan in London, 1865 (courtesy
of the Japan Information and Cultural Centre, London).

government of the new Japan. A group of fifteen Satsuma students similarly
set sail secretly for Britain in 1865 and followed the Choshu path to UCL
where, it has been estimated, some fifty Japanese studied prior to 1880.[29]

Such early Japanese visitors to Europe were sponsored either by the
shogunate or by outward-looking *daimyo*. Formal diplomatic missions were
undertaken to America in 1860, to Europe (as previously described) in
1862, and to France in 1864 and 1867. Shogunate support was extended
to those students sent to Holland from 1866 for the purpose of acquiring a
command of navigational and naval affairs and an understanding of western
governmental systems to aid in Japan's conduct of foreign affairs.[30]

With the advent of the Meiji Restoration (1868), the new Japanese
government mounted a comprehensive mission to Europe and America
in 1871 which was headed by Iwakura Tomomi accompanied by Ito
Hirobumi in the role of Vice-Minister. Its political purpose was to seek
revision of the 'unequal treaties' but its wider agenda was to systematically
amass a wealth of knowledge from the most advanced industrial nations
of the West. In its 18-month-long tour of Europe and America, the
Iwakura mission fulfilled its fact-finding mission admirably. On returning
home in 1873, the emissaries applied their new-found knowledge to the
remodelling of Japan.

Like their *Bakufu* predecessors of 1862, the members of the Iwakura
mission found much to learn from in the European and American cities
which they visited. A detailed record of their travels and impressions

Markino Yoshio, View of Buckingham Palace from Green Park, woodblock print, *c*1910 (Victoria & Albert Museum).

was kept by their Chief Secretary, Kume Kunitake, who compiled a five-volume journal of the mission.

The European itinerary included tours of Britain, France, Belgium, Holland, Germany, Russia, Denmark, Sweden, Italy, Austria and Switzerland. War in Spain prevented the emissaries from extending the mission to Spain and Portugal. By far the longest period of time (from August to December 1872) was spent in Britain, partly for reasons of international diplomacy and partly due to Britain's industrial reputation. This was very much confirmed by the findings of Kume's journal which was based on visits to a wide range of factories and facilities up and down the country.

National and regional differences were observed with perspicacity and candour. Closely paraphrasing from the journal, one author summed up its comparative analysis:

> Europe may be divided at the Alps into an industrious, prosperous north and an indolent impoverished south. England, with her modern steam machinery, mining, railroads, and marine fleet, 'swaggers fearlessly in the world'. French manufacturing is highly developed, and France is the arbiter of artistic taste and luxury for all Europe. Germany has the impressive Krupp armaments works. Even the small nations such as Holland and Belgium are formidable in their industrial and commercial sophistication. The southern countries, in contrast, are backward. Italy still relies on handicraft industry

for a large part of the national outcome and in Spain and
Portugal conditions are yet worse.[31]

Further distinctions were made between the various nations of Europe
based on climate and topography and their influence on national character
and temperament:

France and England, because of their infertile soil, rigorous
climate, and (natural) deficiency in all things, have exerted
strenuous efforts and produced the brilliance of civilisation . . .

In 'tropical countries' by contrast:

there is nothing to produce the desire for knowledge, no need
to endure hardships and undertake enterprises . . . the world
merely passes them by.[32]

Finally, finding a common ground of industriousness with their erstwhile
trading partner:

If people with the minds of the Dutch lived in the lands
of China, one knows that hundreds of Hollands would be
produced in the East.[33]

Throughout the journal, great weight is attached to the role of industry
and commerce in economic and social development. This theme was
frequently addressed in the embassy's progress across Europe:

Even when we had audiences with emperors, kings, and
queens, when we were entertained by foreign ministers,
these two words (commerce and industry) always appeared
in their speeches. As we travelled, commercial and industrial
companies in each city vied with each other to welcome us.
There were banquets overflowing with delicacies. . . . Each
time a speech was made to the crowds, when there was talk
of friendly relations with our country and flourishing trade, all
threw up their hats and stamped their feet.[34]

The potential of Japan as an important market in the East was clearly
acknowledged by each of the countries visited.

The findings of the Iwakura mission threw up lessons for Japan that
were to occupy the Meiji leaders for many years to come. Government
policy underwent change as a result of the mission and the sources for
the continuing modernization of Japan were accordingly adapted following
this first-hand in-depth experience of the West.

The Iwakura mission contributed to the collective national consciousness of Europe in Japan. Kume's journal was published in Japan in 1878
and, along with Samuel Smiles's *Self-Help* (translated in 1871), and Jules
Verne's *Around the World in Eighty Days* (translated in 1878), it enhanced
Britain's image as an industrial giant, an empire inspired to greatness by the

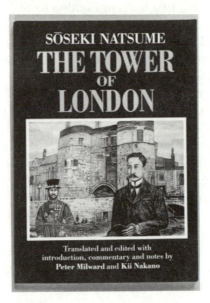

Translated edition of Soseki Natsume's
'The Tower of London' (*Rondon To*),
first published in 1905 (courtesy of In
Print Publishing).

Victorian work ethic, and a nation – in the caricature of Phileas Fogg – of
delightfully eccentric gentlemen.[35]

At the time of the Iwakura mission, it was estimated that there were
nearly 100 Japanese students living in London.[36] In subsequent years,
Japanese artists, writers and intellectuals of various persuasions made
their way to London and to other European capitals motivated by the
modernization and westernization of Japan. For the solitary emigré, the
transition to life in the West was not always an easy one.

The artist Markino Yoshio (1868–1956) came to London in 1897,
working initially in the office of the Japanese naval attaché, and then
struggling to make ends meet until he established himself as an atmospheric
painter of London scenes. Markino, the confirmed Anglophile, wrote
his autobiographical *A Japanese Artist in London* in 1910 and went on
to develop a successful career which was brought to an abrupt halt by
his repatriation back to Japan in 1942. His lengthy residency abroad did
not contribute to contemporary images in Meiji times but is nevertheless
revealing of the wider Japanese intercourse with Europe.

The novelist Soseki Natsume (1867–1916) was the first Japanese scholar
specializing in English literature who was sent to study in Britain by the

Meiji government.[37] His two years in London from 1900 to 1902 were not happy ones but are considered important in that they came at a formative point in his career. His first novel, *Rondon To* (*The Tower of London*) (1905), based on this period in London, established his early reputation in Japan.

These two contrasting experiences not only say something of the adaptive abilities of individuals to foreign lifestyles but of the qualitative differences in the experiences of those Japanese who ventured forth to Europe in the wake of Japan's reopening to the West. Literary historians have further contrasted Soseki's lonely time in London with the four happy years from 1884 spent by the writer, Mori Ogai, as a medical student residing in German university towns.[38] The anonymity of life in a capital city versus the greater accessibility of the provincial town must have also influenced judgements and perceptions of Europe in the early days of student travel.

The Japanese view of Europe was thus a complex composite of so many disparate factors and second-hand impressions derived, at least in part, from those Europeans who had come to Japan and those Japanese who travelled abroad.

But what of the impact made by the reopening of Japan upon Europe? The response of West to East over this same period was one of fascination, and has likewise bequeathed some lingering stereotypes.

From the 1850s onwards, reports of internal conflict and change in Japan as well as western attempts to promote trade appeared with increasing regularity in the European press. As the foreign treaty ports were opened, descriptions of the country written by diplomats and traders conveyed a host of exotic and even disturbing impressions of this far-flung land. Travellers' tales extended the repertoire of images while tending to reaffirm the prejudices brought from home.

Many writers stressed the differences and oppositions which made Japan unique. In the 1860s, Britain's first head of legation, Sir Rutherford Alcock, gave vent to such feelings:

> Japan is essentially a country of anomalies, where all – even familiar things – put on new faces, and are curiously reversed. Except that they do not walk on their heads instead of their feet, there are few things in which they do not seem, by some occult law, to have been impelled in a perfectly opposite direction and a reversed order. They write from top to bottom, from right to left, in perpendicular instead of horizontal lines; and their books begin where ours end. . . . Their locks, though imitated from Europe, are all made to lock by turning the key from left to right . . . Their day is for the most part

1 Christmas and Coca Cola in Japan. The all-pervasive influence of American culture dates back to the Occupation years (1945–52) (Japan Information and Cultural Centre).

2 Britain's Prime Minister, John Major, leads Canadian Prime Minister, Brian Mulroney, and Japanese Prime Minister, Kaifu Toshiki, through the Tower of London during the July 1991 G–7 Summit (Japan Information and Cultural Centre).

3 A youthful Prince Charles accompanied by Morita Akio, Sony Chairman, at the official opening of Sony's Bridgend plant in Wales, December 1973 (Sony Manuf. Co., UK).

4 Prime Minister Margaret Thatcher with Nissan President, Ishihara Takashi, at the official opening of Nissan Motor Manufacturing (UK) Ltd, Sunderland, September 1986 (Nissan Motor Manufacturing UK Ltd).

5 'Japanese Investment in the UK: the European Dimension', an Anglo–Japanese Economic Institute and Scottish Development Agency conference addresses Japan's place in Europe, 1990.

6 World leaders assemble at the Group of Seven Summit in London, July 1991, where the Japan–EC Joint Declaration of Political Friendship was launched (Japan Information and Cultural Centre).

7 The groundbreaking ceremony for Toyota Motor Manufacturing (UK) Ltd's Derbyshire plant, 4 June 1990. L–R: Numata Junji, Chairman, TMUK; Toyoda Eiji, Chairman Toyota Motor Corp; Nicholas Ridley, Secretary of State for Trade and Industry; and Japanese Ambassador to the UK, Chiba Kazuo (Japan Information and Cultural Centre).

9 *Eikoku*, 'The Japanese Magazine on Britain'. A variety of anglocentric Japanese-language publications foster a touristic image of Britain.

8 The Japanese department store, *Sogo*, opened in London's Piccadilly Circus in 1992 (MCH).

10 A Japanese bookshop in London displays the many Japanese books written about Britain and British life (MCH).

11 *Isetan London* stands among Old Bond Street's fashionable boutiques (MCH).

12 Students of Teikyo University of Japan in Durham mingle with their Durham University peers (Teikyo University).

night and this principle of antagonism creeps up in the most unexpected and bygone way in all their moral being, customs and habits.[39]

For some, the 'contrariness' of Japanese ways was more than made up for by the artistic sensibilities of the nation and the simple refinement of the art products that made their way into Europe. Alcock provided the British public with its first organized display of Japanese art at the International Exhibition of 1862 where his own collection was on view. Such exhibitions served as a platform for disseminating a knowledge of Japanese material culture within Europe. In Paris, the Expositions Universelles of 1867, 1878 and 1889 featured more extensive Japanese displays and, at the Vienna International Exhibition of 1873, enthusiasm for the arts and crafts of Japan was further fuelled. It is ironic that the members of the Iwakura mission, Iwakura Tomomi and Ito Hirobumi, in Vienna at the time of the Exhibition, were to focus their attention on the modern products of European innovation rather than the traditional artefacts sent from home.[40] It was not the first, nor would it be the last, time that the Japanese self-image and the European perception of Japan would conflict in the same setting.

Impressions of Japan were much influenced by the artefacts that began pouring into the shops and showrooms of her trading partners in Europe following the reopening of the country. Woodblock prints, painted screens, textiles, porcelain and other goods brought the bold decorative formulae and calligraphic movement specific to the arts of Japan into the European frame. Artists in Paris were the first to be seized with Japan fever. Baudelaire coined the term '*japonaiserie*' in 1861, pointing to the superficial references to Japan and Japanese art. It was not until 1872, however, that the art critic Philippe Burty defined '*japonisme*' with reference to the deeper reflection of Japanese design principles in French art of the period. Certainly the subject matter of Japanese prints was alluded to in the landscapes and figure studies of Manet, Monet, Degas and their contemporaries and, by the 1880s, Van Gogh, Gauguin, Lautrec and others were employing formal devices that truly echoed the aesthetics of Japanese art.

The interest in Japan in French artistic circles was further reflected in the monthly dinners of the Société Japonaise du Jing-lar, an informal 'club' of Japan enthusiasts formed in 1867. The First Congress of Orientalists was held in Paris in 1875 and, in 1888, the art dealer Samuel Bing launched the periodical, *Le Japon Artistique*, which for the next three years furnished its readership with monthly insights into Japanese art.

When Pierre Loti's novel, *Madame Chrysanthème*, was published in

Henri de Toulouse Lautrec, Poster for
the *Divan Japonais*, colour lithograph,
1893 (Victoria & Albert Museum).

France in 1887, it evoked an exotic image of Japan that inspired a
generation of artists and writers and that has long remained in the
forefront of the European imagination. The character Chrysanthème is,
by Loti's definition, a *japonaiserie* come to life:

> As a mere outline, little Chrysanthème has been seen every-
> where and by everybody. Whoever has looked at one of those
> paintings on china or on silk that now fill our bazaars, knows
> by heart the pretty stiff headdress, the leaning figure, ever
> ready to try some new gracious salutation, the scarf fastened
> behind in an enormous bow, the large falling sleeves, the dress
> slightly clinging about the ankles with a little crooked train like
> a lizard's tail.[41]

This same 'outline' was paid homage to by the artists of the Aesthetic
Movement in Britain as the cult of Japan spread outwards from Paris. James
McNeill Whistler was a key figure in preaching the gospel of Japanese
decorative art in Victorian Britain and in introducing its simplicity of form
to a generation of designers. Christopher Dresser whose book, *Japan, Its
Architecture, Art and Art Manufactures* (1882), was based on his travels to
Japan is but one of many British designers who successfully borrowed
from Japanese aesthetic principles. From the 1890s, artists of the Vienna

Secession and the Art Nouveau movement were introducing elements of Japanese taste into the design products of Austria, Germany, Belgium and many other parts of Europe.

European images of Japan following the reopening to trade derived from these sources and many others. In theatre and in music, in art and in literature, the singular, the exotic, the nature-loving and naive faces of Japan were viewed through the looking glass of European preconceptions. The Victorian poet, Edwin Arnold, relayed his first impressions of Japan in 1891 to a Tokyo audience:

> Japan appears to me as close an approach to Lotus-land as I shall ever find. By many a pool of water-lilies and in fairy-like gardens, amid the beautiful rural scenery of Kama-kura or Nikko; under long avenues of cryptomeria; in weird and dreamy Shinto shrines; on the white matting of the teahouses; in the bright bazaars; by your sleeping lakes, and under your stately mountains, I have felt further removed than ever before from the flurry and vulgarity of our European life.[42]

Arnold might just as well have been looking at his surroundings with one eye closed for, by 1891, the application of 'western technology, Japanese values' had brought about changes in Japan that were not even hinted at in his selective observations. Indeed, his Japanese audience balked at the 'pitiless condemnation' his words conveyed.[43]

A contrasting perspective was put forward by another Briton, Basil Hall Chamberlain, writing in 1904:

> Old Japan is dead and gone, and Young Japan reigns in its stead, as opposed in appearance and in aims to its predecessor as history shows many a youthful prince to have been to the late king, his father. The steam-whistle, the newspaper, the voting paper, the pillar post at every streetcorner and even in remote villages, the clerk in shop or bank or public office hastily summoned from our side to answer the ring of the telephone bell, the railway replacing the palanquin, the iron-clad replacing the war-junk, – these and a thousand other startling changes testify that Japan is transported ten thousand miles away from her former moorings.[44]

By the time Chamberlain's volume, *Things Japanese*, was published, Japan had successfully negotiated the revision of the 'unequal treaties', emerged victorious from the Sino-Japanese War of 1894–5, become allied to Britain in the Anglo-Japanese Alliance of 1902 and engaged in a major conflict with Russia. Her victory in the Russo-Japanese War of 1904–5 proved a turning-point in the relationship with Europe and heightened the Japanese concern with how they were viewed in the West. The legacy of Meiji modernization was to place Japan on an equal footing with the major European powers. This was to have consequences for both her image and her future as patronizing delight in the Japan of *Madame Butterfly* gave way to ominous forecasts of an industrial and military rival emerging in the East.

The early encounters between Japan and Europe derived from the culture of trade. From the arrival of the Portuguese in 1543 to the reopening of Japan to the West in 1854, European and American commercial interests prompted the initial overtures from which more complex associations have sprung. The coming together of different cultures and different values is a heady process. This was the case in Japan's Christian and Dutch centuries and in the Meiji era and is no less so today.

2 The Road to 1992: Japan and the European Community

When the Single European Act was agreed in December 1985, Japan was at a crossroads in her relationship with Europe. The notion of 'Europe'as a single corporate entity may have had some distant historical precedent in the eighteenth century when western learning entered Japan via the one channel of the Dutch. A very different view of Europe, however, was established by the end of the Meiji period (1912) during which Japan, the 'rational shopper', had so carefully selected the best and most appropriate models to assist in her modernization and industrialization. The Bakufu mission of 1862 to Europe and the Iwakura mission of 1871 particularly contributed to an awareness of distinct national and regional identities. Britain, France and Germany were the countries from which Japan borrowed most heavily during these years, and the subsequent history of economic relations with Europe was to be similarly influenced by such bilateral ties.

The First World War accelerated the pace of industrial development in Japan. By 1914, the silk and cotton textile industries had become central to her economic growth. Wartime disruption of British, French and German trade enabled Japan to gain new export markets in the East and to greatly expand the capacity of her merchant marine which more than doubled between 1914 and 1918.[1] The war gave rise too to the diversification of industry, as Japanese munitions factories and shipyards stepped up production to meet the needs of western allies. Indigenous needs also prompted the development of particular sectors, as with the chemical industry which had previously relied on imports from Germany but which later came to be locally sourced.[2] Japan's dependence on imported raw materials was heightened with the growth of heavy industry in the inter-war period. Between 1920 and 1940, the volume of iron and steel production increased eleven times and machinery and chemical production six times, while textile output up to 1935 nearly trebled.[3] Continued export growth financed the demands of heavy industry as markets gained in the war were retained and strengthened. By 1929, raw silk and cotton goods accounted for two-thirds of the export trade with Japan's key textile markets located in the United States, India and China.[4] The raw materials shortage fuelled colonialist expansion in East Asia during these years which was done in the name of economic necessity and against the backdrop of the protectionist mood of the 1920s.

The Anglo-Japanese Alliance had come to an end following the Washington Conference of 1921–2 and the agreement of the Four Power Pact (1921) involving Britain, Japan, France and the United States. As Japan's special relationship with Britain lapsed, the postwar economic slump made for further changes on the world stage. Ideals of international cooperation and economic growth through peaceful competition gave way to export dumping, tariff barriers and protectionism. The path to war was paved with the demise of the free trade system.

Japanese colonialist aggression in China in the 1930s eventually led to economic repercussions as the United States placed embargoes on oil, iron and steel exports in 1940 and, in 1941, initiated what was virtually a total western embargo on trade. The events leading up to the attack on Pearl Harbor are well known. Japan's war plans, which called for the creation of a Greater East Asian Co-Prosperity Sphere, represented a complete turning away from the West and, through economic and military domination, the substitution of a 'New Order of East Asia'. The failure of these plans was, ironically, to result in the full-scale American domination of Japan in the postwar period.

Japan's relationship with the United States has been the central plank of her foreign policy since the Second World War. This orientation towards America dates back to the Occupation years (1945–52) when political and constitutional reform and industrial restructuring were executed under the auspices of the Supreme Commander for the Allied Powers (SCAP).

The demilitarization and democratization of Japan were the stated aims of the Occupation forces. Allied involvement as such was greatly limited, however, both bureaucratically and militarily. The British Commonwealth Occupation Force consisted of 40,000 men compared with a US force of 250,000.[5] By 1948 the Allied troops had left Japan in the complete control of the Americans.

To all intents and purposes, then, Japan was dominated by American policy during the Occupation years and her future relationship with America was sealed through the terms of the US–Japan Security Treaty of 1952. The ongoing American presence in Japan ensured that her perspectives on the West would be American- rather than European-led. The cultural manifestations of this orientation, from baseball to Kentucky Fried Chicken, are still in evidence today.

Japan's rise from the ashes following demilitarization and the further enactment of labour, land and educational reforms were greatly aided by events in Korea. The outbreak of the Korean War in 1950 provided a direct stimulus to economic recovery as Japanese industry faced up to the immediate challenge of filling military equipment orders for United Nations forces and procurement orders for American bases in Japan. By 1955 the process of reconstruction was overtaken by genuine expansion and a period of sustained growth.

Japan's industrial infrastructure had been devastated by the war. The Occupation reforms were intended to implement a more democratic industrial framework to replace the large industrial conglomerates or *zaibatsu* that had orchestrated Japanese military expansion. Despite the passing of the Anti-Monopoly Law in April 1947 to limit the revival of such groupings, as demand increased in the 1950s, Japan's industrial giants re-emerged as a dominant force.

Japan's economic revival has been attributed to a number of factors including the close relationship between government and industry.[6] The Ministry of International Trade and Industry (MITI) was established in 1949 and has since played a key role in the management of industrial strategy and trade. Government support for industry coupled with the strengths of Japan's enterprise culture brought a country on the brink of economic collapse in 1945 once more to its feet. Japan Inc. became the pseudonym for a national outlook of corporate values in which all were united as one.

In the aftermath of the Second World War, the restoration of trade proved a more elusive goal to attain. Japan's application in 1951 to join the General Agreement on Tariffs and Trade (GATT) was rejected, largely through lingering resentments and fears that she would flood European markets with cheap goods. US support played an important part in her eventual re-entry to the international economic community. Admission to the International Monetary Fund and the International Bank of Reconstruction and Development in 1952 was followed by the acceptance of Japan's application to join GATT in 1955. The latter was seen as only a partial victory, however, for Britain, France, Belgium and the Netherlands (as well as ten other countries) invoked Article 35 and, in doing so, withheld 'most-favoured nation' status from her. Japan's re-entry to the world club was consequently restricted in terms that may well have seemed, to some, reminiscent of the 'unequal treaties' of the previous century.

The Japanese postwar 'economic miracle' saw the industrial production index leap from 84 in 1950 to 410 in 1960.[7] The 13.2 per cent growth rate achieved in 1960 was to set the standard for a decade of continued economic expansion. The development of heavy industry and advances in the manufacturing sector, particularly in the fields of chemicals and engineering, created new strengths and new markets. Japan's production and export of ships, cameras, automobiles and man-made fibres in the 1960s established her reputation as a supplier of advanced industrial goods. In 1965, the first trade surplus was registered since the Second World War, starting a trend which was to be maintained until a currency crisis and international pressure brought about the re-evaluation of the yen in 1971. The intervening years heightened the miraculous transformation of the economy as the gross national product (GNP) surpassed first that of Italy in 1966, the UK in 1967, France in 1968 and Germany in 1969.[8]

As Japan was adjusting in the postwar period to new circumstances and international ties, the nations of Europe were undergoing economic realignment as part of the reconstruction process. The European Community was established in 1957 out of an organizational framework created by the 1951 Treaty of Paris and the 1957 Treaties of Rome. Its components and forerunners were the European Coal and Steel Community, the European Economic Community and the European Atomic Energy Community. The purpose of the European Community was the revitalization of the European economy by market integration and the harmonization of external tariffs. The original signatories were Belgium, France, the Federal Republic of Germany, Italy, Luxemburg and the Netherlands. The United Kingdom, Denmark and the Republic of Ireland were admitted as members in 1973 followed by Greece in 1981 and Spain and Portugal in 1986.

Japanese fears of an 'exclusionist trading club' in a united Europe had early led to the pursuit of trade negotiations with individual European countries.[9] A series of bilateral agreements concluded with the UK, Benelux countries and France between 1962 and 1963 extended 'most-favoured nation' status to Japan. In their wake, the European Commission began moves to establish a common trade policy towards Japan. It was on the issue of cotton import quotas that an initial agreement between the European Community and Japan was reached in June 1969.[10]

Japan's ambiguous attitude to the European Community has been attributed to a preference for dealing with the individual nations of Europe on the grounds of 'familiarity, tradition, the emotional factor, and organizational considerations'.[11] Certainly, the replacement of established relationships and networks going back to Meiji times with the perceived multilateral bureaucratic machine of the European Community led the Japanese to continue to press for negotiations with each member state on a separate basis. As trading frictions accelerated in the 1970s and 80s, EC–Japan relations were to develop and evolve.

Japan's trade with Europe increased from the 1960s with the UK's position as leading export market being gradually overtaken by that of Germany. Early exports of labour-intensive light industrial products, such as textiles, clothing and toys, were superseded by a whole range of sophisticated manufactured goods from consumer electronics to cars.[12] Changes in Japan's industrial structure were reflected in the ever-increasing trade surplus with Europe from the early 1970s. The pattern of importing manufactured goods from Europe while exporting raw materials and light industrial goods was essentially reversed as more than 90 per cent of Japan's exports to Europe came to consist of manufactured goods.[13]

Exports to the European Community increased ten times in value between 1970 and 1980 while exports from the EC to Japan were to rise by only five times over this same period.[14] The imposition of import restrictions by the United States and the devaluation of the dollar in 1971 had shifted Japan's gaze from America to Europe. The 1973 oil shock further exacerbated this trend so that, by 1975, EC exports to Japan had dropped to just 40 per cent of her imports from Japan.[15]

Japan's export drive on Europe and the resulting trade surpluses prompted a number of *ad hoc* bilateral measures to stem the tide. Voluntary export restraints on various commodities were introduced and a series of anti-dumping investigations forced up the export prices of such products as bearings. Despite these attempts to right the balance of trade, between 1970 and 1976 the flow of exports from Japan to the European Community increased fourfold.[16]

EC–Japan trade frictions reached fever-pitch in October of 1976 as mounting unemployment in Europe and a record trade deficit with Japan formed the backdrop to a Japanese industrial mission to Europe. The mission, headed by Doko Toshio, President of the Keidanren (Federation of Economic Organizations), faced heated criticisms wherever they went of Japanese unfair practices in the five 'problem sectors' of steel, ships, home electronics, bearings and cars.[17] Upon his return to Japan, Doko pressed the government into action. Japan's time-honoured preoccupation with her image in the West and the loss of face engendered by the direct challenge put to the mission members combined to produce a quick response on the part of the Japanese authorities.

Measures were taken to curb exports in the specified controversial sectors but also to facilitate an increase of European imports into Japan. Information exchange and the raising of public awareness of trade issues were accomplished as a result of this episode of Japan bowing to foreign pressure. While trade crises continued to occur, as with the aftermath of the second oil shock of 1979, the 'Doko shock' of 1976 can nevertheless be credited with bringing the EC–Japan trade problem into the public arena.

It has been argued that the Doko visit provided the European Community with an opportunity to politicize the trade dispute and to thus force Japan into recognizing the EC as a corporate body, 'not as a legal fiction but as an actually existing entity'.[18] Certainly it began the process of establishing a dialogue between Japan and the EC which was to be taken forward with the 'Poitiers incident' of 1982. The shifting Japanese perspectives on the European Community versus Europe remained a background theme through the trade frictions that followed.

Japan responded to the second oil shock of 1979 by mounting a renewed export drive on Europe. Its impact was dramatic with exports to the European Community rising between 1979 and 1981 by almost 60 per cent.[19] European countermeasures included the institution of statistical surveillance of imports on Japanese cars, televisions and machine tools in 1981 and the systematic increase in anti-dumping proceedings against Japanese imports throughout the 1980s.

An EC Commission Report, leaked to the press in the spring of 1979, personalized the trade debate with its contentious references to the Japanese as 'workaholics' living in 'rabbit hutches'. The backlash in Japan was immediate and sharp. Japan's relationship with the European Community was further tested during these years by mounting pressures from the individual member states. France had been the last European trading partner to grant 'most-favoured nation' status to Japan in 1963 and protectionist measures had subsequently limited the scale of Japanese imports into the country. The much-quoted 'Poitiers incident' saw the French responding tactically to an unwelcome influx of videocassette recorders (VCRs) in 1982. By requiring all VCR imports to undergo clearance at the remote customs office of Poitiers, restricted entry of Japanese goods into France was achieved.[20] While in contravention of all the rules of GATT, France's 'go-slow' ploy and the role played by the European Commission in the negotiations that followed, pointed up to the Japanese that problems of international trade might best be handled through the central mechanism of the EC.[21]

The alleviation of trade frictions through direct access to an integrated market in Europe was a prime factor in generating the 'great wave' of

Japanese direct investment into the EC in the 1980s. Japanese trading companies had established an early presence in Europe in the postwar period, setting up branch offices and sales and distribution networks in their major export markets from the 1950s. By the mid-1970s, it has been calculated that Japan's five leading trading companies – Mitsui & Co., Mitsubishi Corp., Marubeni Corp., C.Itoh & Co., and Sumitomo SK – 'accounted for more than 40 per cent of the total overseas investment of Japan's top fifty firms'.[22] Their emphasis on exporting revolved around the procurement of raw materials to aid in Japan's reconstruction and development and the establishing of a marketing network to facilitate trade. The former activity was concentrated in Asia while the latter was predominantly pursued in North America and Europe. This same marketing and information-gathering network later supplied an inbuilt international infrastructure for manufacturing firms investing overseas. Japanese banks and insurance companies which likewise came to Europe in these early years provided essential support services to augment the activities of the trading firms.

Japanese foreign direct investment in the early postwar period was almost negligible, given the restrictions on outflows of foreign reserves and, until 1971, the virtual dependence of companies upon specific government approval to invest.[23] Indeed, during these years, the low cost of labour in Japan provided little incentive to set up overseas operations. Towards the end of the 1960s, however, the rising value of the yen along with shortages and increased costs for labour and raw materials began to alter government policy and to stimulate foreign investment.[24]

Trade frictions between Japan and Europe in subsequent years were focused, as has been indicated, upon particular problem sectors such as motor vehicles and consumer electronics in the 1970s and, additionally, videocassette recorders, photocopiers and semiconductors in the 1980s.[25] By 1984 Japan was producing 44 per cent of the world's consumer electronic products and 90 per cent of the videocassette recorders.[26] The ongoing application of export restraints to these goods increased the desirability for the Japanese of establishing bases in Europe to enable manufacturers to conduct trade from within.

The internationalization of Japanese industry proceeded apace from the 1970s in direct parallel to conflicts over trade. Sony Corp. was a pioneer investor in the UK with its colour television factory, opened at Bridgend in South Wales in 1974, and Canon Inc. established the first Japanese manufacturing investment in France when it opened its photocopier factory at Rennes in Brittany in 1984. The establishment of Nissan Motor Manufacturing (UK) Ltd at Washington in the North of England in 1984 represented the largest-ever investment in Europe by a Japanese firm.

The massive appreciation of the yen against the dollar following the Plaza Accord of 1985 and the signing of the Single European Act in that same year gave a particular impetus to Japanese manufacturing investment in Europe. The 1980s bubble economy produced positive internal and external environments, conducive to growth and the enhancement of already healthy markets for Japanese goods. In 1986, the report of the Maekawa Commission which was set up to improve trade relations was published. In it, recommendations were made to reduce Japan's dependence on exports by various means including the more than doubling of outward direct investment as a percentage of gross domestic product (GDP) by 1992.[27] The rising numbers of Japanese manufacturing operations in Europe from 18 in 1970 to 123 in 1980 and 516 in 1990 provide statistical evidence of the trend established by these combined forces.[28]

Japanese direct investment overseas had peaked by 1990 as a deepening recession greatly decreased the availability of capital for corporate developments abroad. With the changed domestic climate following the bursting of the bubble and with the weakened state of the European economy, the expansionist mood of the 1980s gave way to a spirit of caution. Planning for profit replaced the growth-led strategies of the past. Real estate investment especially suffered as the world-wide recession hit the overseas ventures of Japan's new-age buccaneers. Between 1990 and 1993 alone the share of real estate investment totals dropped from 19.5 per cent to 12.5 per cent.[29]

While finance and the services have traditionally dominated Japanese direct investment in Europe, manufacturing assumed an increasingly prominent place from the mid-1980s, growing from less than 10 per cent of all Japanese FDI in the European Community in 1985 to more than 23 per cent in 1993.[30] The pattern of Japanese manufacturing investment in Europe and North America in the sectors of electrical and electronic machinery, transport equipment and general machinery has mirrored that of Japanese exports. Japan's exporting experience in particular geographical regions has provided companies with localized knowledge of market factors and consumer taste which has smoothed the ground for follow-up investments.[31]

As Japanese manufacturing strategies shifted in the mid-1980s from export orientation to a focus on local production, the share of both cumulative and manufacturing investment in the European Community greatly increased. Consequently, some twenty countries of Europe have played host, with varying degrees of enthusiasm, to a wide range of

Note: Figures represent the number of manufacturing firms in which Japanese companies have an interest of 10% or more.

Source: JETRO centres and offices in Europe.

Map showing the location of Japanese manufacturers in Europe as of January 1994 (JETRO).

34

	January 1985	January 1987	December 1987	January 1989	January 1990	January 1991	January 1992	January 1993	January 1994
UK	32	53	68	91	129	175	189	197	206
France	30	33	38	81	89	106	115	119	121
Germany	35	46	54	65	87	99	106	108	106
Netherlands	16	20	19	27	33	36	44	46	45
Belgium	15	18	19	23	25	32	38	38	40
Luxembourg					2	2	3	3	3
Ireland	11	10	12	19	22	26	30	30	31
Spain	22	29	33	41	54	64	63	63	64
Italy	8	11	15	24	28	38	45	45	52
Finland	2	2	2	2	4	4	4	5	5
Norway	2	2	2	1	0	0	1	1	1
Sweden	1	1	3	6	6	69	9	10	
Denmark	2	2	2	2	3	3	3	3	3
Austria	2	5	5	7	12	14	15	17	17
Portugal	7	6	6	7	13	13	13	12	12
Switzerland	0	1	1	4	5	7	7	9	8
Greece	4	4	4	4	3	3	3	3	3
Iceland	0	0	0	0	1	1	1	1	1
Total	189	243	283	404	516	629	689	709	728
Increase from previous year		54	40	121	112	113	60	20	19
Change from previous year (%)		28.6	16.5	42.8	27.7	21.9	9.5	2.9	2.7

Note: Some data of previous surveys are revised

a   Japanese manufacturers by country (excluding independent R&D facilities)

a and b   Japanese manufacturers and R&D facilities in Europe as of January 1994 (JETRO).

	January 1990	January 1991	January 1992	January 1993	January 1994
UK	24 (9)	47 (14)	72 (18)	79 (20)	83 (19)
France	10 (3)	17 (6)	29 (8)	33 (10)	34 (8)
Germany	14 (6)	28 (11)	38 (13)	46 (19)	53 (18)
Netherlands	3	4	6 (1)	12 (3)	16 (4)
Belgium	4 (1)	8 (2)	10 (3)	17 (5)	16 (4)
Luxembourg					
Ireland	1	2 (1)	2 (1)	5 (1)	7 (1)
Spain	11	15	23	20 (2)	26 (2)
Italy	3 (2)	8 (1)	8 (2)	12 (3)	14 (4)
Finland	0	0	1	1	0
Norway	0	0	1	1	1
Sweden	1	1	3	5 (1)	5 (1)
Denmark	0	1 (1)	1 (1)	1 (1)	1 (1)
Austria	0	0	2 (1)	5	3
Portugal	0	0	0	0	0
Switzerland	1 (1)	3 (3)	3 (3)	3 (2)	4 (3)
Greece	0	0	0	0	0
Iceland	0	1	1	0	1
Total	72 (22)	135 (39)	200 (51)	240 (67)	264 (65)
Increase from previous year		63 (17)	65 (12)	40 (16)	24 (-2)

b R&D facilities (of which, independent facilities)

Japanese firms and the infrastructure for Japanese investment – since the arrival of trading companies and financial institutions in the 1950s and 1960s – has burgeoned.

The value of Japanese cumulative investment in Europe at the end of 1993 amounted to US$79,609 million, representing a 19.6 per cent share of Japan's total direct investment abroad.[32] Not surprisingly, such investment has been drawn to those parts of Europe with a substantial financial and services infrastructural base; the UK leads Europe with a 8.6 per cent share of Japan's cumulative foreign direct investment as calculated in 1992, followed by the Netherlands with 4.2 per cent and Germany with 2.3 per cent. Relative to Japanese investment in Europe, each country's percentage share is, of course, considerably higher.

The importance of Japanese manufacturing investment in Europe is calculated not only on the basis of total project value (set at US$17,331 million as of the end of 1993) but also in relation to wider benefits ranging from the creation of direct and indirect employment and technology exchange. For this reason, the last decade has witnessed the considerable wooing of the Japanese by various European governments. For others, it must be said, the Japanese move into Europe will ever be identified with the progress of a 'trojan horse'.

As of January 1994, a total of 728 Japanese manufacturers were operating in Europe with the largest share of such investment in the UK (206 cases), France (121), Germany (106) and Spain (64). The geographical disposition of manufacturing investment has been determined by a number of factors, both strategic and cultural, and by the public relations role played by governments and development agencies in the selection process.

The scrutinizing of national and regional infrastructures and communications networks in relation to the needs of particular industries has led investors into different corners of Europe. The excellent port facilities of Barcelona, for example, and the high standard of Schipol Airport at Amsterdam have been frequently cited as reasons for investing in Spain and the Netherlands respectively.

Access to the required quality and quantity of 'cheap' labour have influenced other location decisions. One Japanese consumer–electronics manufacturer inadvertently boosted Britain's investment image by citing the salary level of his company's West German shop floor workers as twice that of his Welsh employees.[33]

Along with labour cost and availability, the issue of labour relations is of paramount concern to the Japanese. A three-and-a-half-month-long strike at Suzuki's Santana plant in Andalusia in 1994 has inevitably had an adverse effect on Japanese attitudes towards investment in Spain. While some would place the blame for the strike on regional factors, attention drawn to such human relations problems can work to the broader detriment of future investment. Language and communication difficulties exacerbated already strained management–labour relations at Santana and served to point up another requirement of the Japanese working overseas. With English as the second language of most company employees, the ability to conduct business in English, as is possible in the UK, Netherlands and other northern European countries, is seen as a positive advantage.

These then are some of the practical considerations facing the Japanese as they look towards Europe. The receptivity of different European countries to Japanese investment, or the 'welcome factor', also plays its part. At a governmental level, comparisons have been made[34] between the UK, Belgium and the Netherlands, who have courted Japanese investment to aid in the regeneration of economically deprived regions, and Ireland, Portugal and Spain for whom Japanese investment has lent impetus to national industrialization drives. France and Italy, on the other hand, have displayed a certain ambivalence, if not downright negativism, towards investment from Japan.

Regional development grants, tax incentives and liaison and support facilities are some of the mechanisms whereby national and regional governments compete with each other to attract the Japanese and other investors. Some would argue that with a certain standardization of financial and other incentives, Europe has become a level playing-field in this regard.

Over the last ten years, as Japanese investment has come to be concentrated in particular countries and regions for logistical and other reasons, a multiplier effect has occurred. The social and cultural infrastructure that has developed around Japanese companies in Europe has become an attraction in itself for new investors.

To a certain extent, the decision to invest in the UK, France, Germany, Spain or the Netherlands is something of a lottery, and the balance can be tipped by personal considerations. The Japanese managing director with a taste for French cuisine or the company president who was in London during his student days may come to influence decisions formulated out of more pragmatic concerns. The power of images and impressions cannot be dismissed or disentangled from the hard economic factors that have guided the Japanese course to Europe in recent years.

There is no single European image of Japan but an amalgam of historical and contemporary reference points from the *japonaiseries* of the nineteenth-century to the 'cheap shoddy' goods of the 'sweat shops' of the 1930s to the high-quality and high-tech consumer electronic products of the last twenty years. The prevalence of physical objects, both artefacts and merchandising products, in the European consciousness of Japan has created a fixed perspective from which to view the country and the people. As distance has limited the scope of first-hand experience, so has the flood of exports from Japan become synonymous with the nation, so often pejoratively described in workaholic terms as makers of things. That the Japanese image of Europe is more multi-dimensional is perhaps the legacy of the Meiji years when 'a tradition of looking at Europe in terms of its discreet building blocks' evolved.[35]

Relations between Japan and Europe in modern times have been informed by overlapping mutual perceptions very often in the context of bilateral economic ties and trade issues. Britain, Germany and France all shared in the past history of Japan's modernization and have more recently contributed individually to the interface of Japan's relationship with the European Community as a whole.

The Japanese have long enjoyed a 'special relationship' with the United Kingdom and have viewed Britain as an ally and an intermediary within the European Community. Following the conclusion of an Anglo-Japanese commercial treaty in 1962 which, it was felt, would secure a friend at court, the Japanese were clearly disconcerted by the French veto of the UK application to join the EEC.[36] Britain became a member of the EEC in 1973 and has subsequently, on a number of occasions, come to the aid of Japan in Europe.

Japanese fears of a 'Fortress Europe' have been somewhat assuaged by Britain's role, for example, in blocking French moves to extend the European local content ratio to Japanese cars made in Britain. The strong stand taken by the British Prime Minister, Margaret Thatcher, in defence of Nissan and other Japanese carmakers in Britain, was applauded by the Japanese who were much reassured by this show of support through mutual self-interest.[37]

Following the Danish referendum, further cracks were detected in 'Fortress Europe' when Britain opted out of the Social Chapter clause of the Maastricht Treaty in 1992. The dictates of the Social Chapter on working hours, conditions of service and the role of unions in corporate management were viewed with apprehension by the Japanese. Britain's Foreign Secretary, Douglas Hurd, was to explain the rejection of the contentious clause with special reference to its potentially negative impact on foreign investors in Britain and particularly the Japanese. Hurd's introduction of the 'Japan card' into the European debate was clearly tied to Britain's premier role in attracting more than 40 per cent of all Japanese investment into Europe.

'Youkoso!' Derbyshire County
Council extends a welcome to
Toyota, May 1990.

The UK government's support for Japanese investment has been a central feature of Anglo-Japanese economic relations and was particularly characteristic of the Thatcher years. Britain ranks first in the EC and second only to the United States in its global share of Japanese foreign direct investment. Margaret Thatcher played a direct part in encouraging Nissan to invest in the UK, 'lifting the portcullis', as some would have it, for a succession of Japanese manufacturers to move into Europe. Impressed with the sophistication of Japanese technology and the possibilities for fusing the Japanese work ethic onto the 'Victorian values' ideology by which she sought to revitalize Britain, Thatcher sounded a clarion call for the Japanization of British industry.

This positive approach to Japan in Britain has extended in recent years to the issue of trade. In 1988, the Trade and Industry Secretary, Lord Young, launched the 'Opportunity Japan' Campaign, the first such export drive in Europe, aimed at doubling Britain's flow of goods into Japan in a three-year period. Its successor, 'Priority Japan', in 1991, focused again on Britain's exports to but also investment in Japan. (The UK ranks third in Europe in the case of the latter.) 'Action Japan' took up the cudgels in 1994 of raising an awareness among British business interests of the opportunities offered up by the Japanese market. Japan's annual trade surplus with Britain of more than US$7 billion remains a cause for concern, but such exercises acknowledge the positive measures that can be taken to increase exports as well as reducing imports in the pursuit of balanced trade.[38]

Germany is Japan's leading trading partner in Europe and has the fourth largest share of European investment in Japan. As Japan's trade surplus with Germany has risen to US$8.2 billion, so too has German anxiety over an imbalance that represents one-third of Japan's surplus with the EC as a whole.[39]

Many outside observers point to a natural affinity between Japan and Germany; both countries were defeated in the Second World War and both have rebuilt their economies to emerge as major global powers. It is a point of comparison which neither chooses to overemphasize. Nevertheless, the present-day economic partnership between Japan and Germany is strong and stable.

Germany enjoys the third largest share of Japanese foreign direct investment, and also Japanese manufacturing investment in Europe, despite Japanese concerns over high labour costs and restrictive labour laws. The Germans have been quick to dismiss such implicit criticism of their labour policy. The Chairman of I.G. Metall, the leading German trade union, put forward his own view of Japanese labour practices: 'To work like the Japanese' he said, 'with their labour conditions and social practices, would be to revert to the stone age'.[40] For the Japanese, high standards of technical training in Germany provide a positive counterbalance to offset such concerns.

Germany's leading role in the European Community has, in recent years, blurred the bilateral relationship with Japan as unreserved support for free trade has given way to more 'EC-like' pronouncements.[41] The reunification of Germany in 1989 altered Japan's outlook on Europe as the removal of the East–West divide prompted a reconsideration of diplomatic and security issues. A united Germany has also opened up new markets, although there has been a disappointed reaction to the slow cautious pace of Japanese investment. In short, the relationship between Japan and Germany has a substantial economic basis but with tensions increasing in direct proportion to the trade imbalance.

There is something of a disproportion between the quantity of French trade with Japan and the amount of rhetoric which it generates. Though France is only Japan's fourth most important trading partner in Europe, her voice is still the loudest to be heard. Ever since General de Gaulle described the Japanese Prime Minister Ikeda, on a visit to Europe in 1962, as an 'electronics salesman', French views of the Japanese have been given a high press profile. The 'Poitiers incident' of 1982 again saw the French engaged in direct conflict with the Japanese. The restriction imposed on

An advertisement by DATAR's Invest in France Network to attract Japanese investors into France.

Japanese car imports to 3 per cent of the French market and the stringent fixing of local content levels for Japanese cars manufactured in the EC have similarly demonstrated the French protectionist response to Japanese trade issues.

France has, on the other hand, joined the race to attract Japanese investment and has the second-largest share of Japanese manufacturing investment in Europe and the fourth largest share of cumulative investment. France is also the fifth-largest European investor in Japan.

The message sent out to potential Japanese investors from central government as opposed to the regions has not always been a consistent one. During the period of Edith Cresson's prime ministerial leadership, from March 1991 to April 1992, the French international development body, DATAR, and its Invest in France (IFN) regional network were proactive in their wooing of the Japanese. French ministerial delegations were similarly committed to this process and were visiting Japan to encourage investment just as Mme Cresson was publicly comparing the Japanese to 'ants' and describing the Japanese market as 'hermetically-sealed'.[42] While Cresson represented an extreme position *vis à vis* Japan, the conflicting signals sent out during her term of office have been echoed in France's ongoing pro-investment yet protectionist policies towards Japan.

Le Japon C'est Possible, France's answer to the 'Opportunity Japan' campaign was launched in January 1992 with the similar aim of trade

* * * THE SUNDAY TELEGRAPH JUNE 23 1991

INTERNATIONAL

War of words wounds Japan

by Robert Whymant
in Tokyo

FEELINGS are running high after French Prime Minister Edith Cresson's description of the Japanese as "little yellow men who sit up all night thinking of ways to screw the Americans and the Europeans."

Police have been posted outside French businesses in Tokyo and the Japanese Foreign Ministry, furious at her intemperate language, summoned France's ambassador to deliver a stiff protest in the sharpest term "without precedent since 1945."

A Tokyo tabloid, stung by Mrs Cresson's comment that "Japan is another universe which wants to conquer", branded most French women as hysterical and even urged its readers to stop buying Louis Vuitton bags.

The Japanese are hurt and puzzled by the warnings that they are bent on domination — echoed in a new CIA-funded study which says it fears Japan's planned economic power is based on a shared national vision for world economic domination.

The charges reflect increasing concern at the leverage that Japan's formidable industrial and financial strength gives it worldwide. With the end of the Cold War, Japan is perceived as a greater threat to America than the Soviet Union, according to opinion polls. Last week, Mrs Cresson

assured Japanese MPs visiting Paris that her criticism was aimed not at Japan's people but its big enterprises. However, the damage had been done.

Far Right groups continue to stage anti-French demonstrations, with a big rally scheduled for July 14. In the eyes of the 120,000 members of ultra-Right groups, Mrs Cresson's remarks come close to a *casus belli*.

"If our relationship with France deteriorates further, both countries will be forced to put national interests first. This could endanger world peace," said Mitsuhiro Kimura, a leader of the Issuikai, a radical Right organisation.

The Society of the Sacred Dragon, another of Japan's 840 extreme Rightwing groups, sent loudspeaker trucks to the French embassy to blast out demands that Mrs Cresson apologise.

Ever suspicious of foreigners' motives, many Japanese are quick to conclude that a hostile world is once again ganging up on them.

"Resurgence of [wartime] feelings of 'Devilish Americans and British' and 'Japanophobia'" was the headline given to an 18-page survey on worsening relations in the middle-brow magazine *AERA* this month. The magazine detects a Japanese backlash to foreign criticism of its "unfair trade practices".

"There are signs of a new nationalism in the hearts of Japanese," says one article. "What can be done about it? That's the task in hand. What we shouldn't do is follow the

path of isolation, like we did 50 years ago."

The *AERA* survey is imbued with the paranoia that is never far below the surface. "Some sections of America believe that they should join hands with Europe to contain Japan, just as Madame Cresson argues for a common front against Japan," it says.

It is hardly surprising that *Japan 2000*, commissioned by the CIA (which has since disavowed itself from the report) should feed Japanese paranoia. For its authors make the claim that Japan is conspiring to use its economic might and propaganda to "impose its culture and values throughout the world".

The accusation is nonsense, according to officials, newspaper editors, and leading academics. "Conquering the world is not on Japan's

agenda," said Mitsuru Uchida, professor of politics at Waseda University. "The problem is that we Japanese swagger around the world flashing our money. We are seen as a people only interested in economics and devoid of any philosophy."

But one Briton, with a restaurant in Tokyo, disagrees. Years of eavesdropping on conversations between middle managers of banks and trading houses has convinced him of one thing. "These people will never rest until they get even with the US for being defeated in 1945. It's a tenet of national faith. If you don't understand this compulsion to humble the Americans, you don't understand the Japanese."

The outbreak of perceived Japanophobia could hardly have come at a worse time. Japanese officials fear that the 50th anniversary of Pearl Harbour, on December 7, will exacerbate anti-Japanese feelings. Their concerns were heightened by last week's announcement that the US would issue commemorative stamps showing American ships sinking after the attack.

Britain could benefit from the wave of Japanophobia spreading in Europe. A Japanese businessman based in London said it made him uneasy to deal with French companies in the present climate, and that Britain should be able to attract an even bigger share of Japanese investment as a result of Mrs Cresson's "insults".

Aera's view: Mitterrand and Delors watch as Edith Cresson fires her barbs at premier Toshiki Kaifu

Provocative: Edith Cresson's 'little yellow men' remarks angered the Japanese

French Prime Minister, Edith Cresson, raised international headlines with her attack upon the Japanese in June 1991.

expansion. Long-standing cultural affinities have seen Japan become the largest export market for French films along with the growth in sales there of French luxury products. The emphasis of the campaign, however, has been on extending the French quality image in Japan from the culture and luxury goods market to that of France's high-technology industries. The active role played in the campaign by French business interests working alongside government has uncovered yet another facet of the French relationship with Japan.

The UK, Germany and France have followed separate paths in their shared histories with Japan yet, as elements within the European Community, each country has contributed to a collective position on Euro-Japanese relations. The Japanese have argued that the dynamic of 'Europe' has led to the adoption of a 'least common denominator' approach in seeking consensus over trade and other issues relevant to the interests of the EC member states.[43] They prefer, as some would suggest, 'to deal bilaterally with each member nation, playing one off against another rather than facing a unified EC'.[44] The 'Cresson factor', with reference to the French Prime Minister's confrontational style of leadership, has, for example, had its positive dimension for the Japanese in the sounding of a discordant note in the symphony of Europe.

European integration has raised the stakes in the overall process of exchange and highlighted the need to put right the imbalance of knowledge as well as of trade with Japan. The differing perspectives from which Europe and Japan view each other was summed up by one (Japanese) commentator writing in 1991:

> Japanese–European relations have up to now been character-
> ized by a cultural infatuation with Europe on Japan's part and
> a lack of interest in Japan on the European side. Ever since
> the Meiji Restoration of 1868 . . . the Japanese have taken
> the countries of Europe as models. But for most Europeans,
> including businesspeople and politicians, Japan has been of little
> concern.[45]

In May 1991, Jacques Delors, as President of the European Community, paid his first visit to Japan since 1986. In the intervening five years, Japan's trade with and investment in the European Community had scaled new heights. But it was the strengthening and broadening of Japan–EC relations that was to dominate Delors's agenda.

The purpose of the Delors visit was to formalize the detail of the Japan–EC Joint Declaration of political friendship that was later launched at the Group of Seven summit in July 1991. Its rationale was elucidated in a Japanese government policy statement:

The relationship between Japan and the EC has not been very close either politically or economically, compared with the Japan–US or the US–EC relationship. Furthermore, public perceptions of the relationship have tended to focus on economic frictions. Given that both Japan and the EC are major industrialised democracies with shared values, there has not been sufficient cooperation between the two.[46]

The 'skewed triangle' of Japan–US–EC relations became the focus of an agreement that has alternately been described as 'a major breakthrough in Japan–EC relations', the weakest side of the triangular grouping, or 'a useful public relations exercise for the Japanese'.

The diversion of attention from the singular issue of the trade imbalance to the wider relationship between Japan and Europe at the critical juncture of 1992 was accomplished through a series of policy statements and recommendations, both broad and specific. A concrete framework for formal consultations was provided for through regular ministerial-level meetings and through annual discussions between the President of the European Council, the President of the Commission and the Japanese Prime Minister. The emphasis on political dialogue underlined the need for the EC and Japan:

> to inform and consult each other on major international issue, which are of common interest to both parties, be they political, economic, scientific, cultural or other. They will strive, whenever appropriate, to coordinate their positions. They will strengthen their cooperation and exchange of information both between the two parties and within international organizations.[47]

As trade relations were subsumed into the diplomatic arena, a programme was outlined to address such areas of mutual concern as international security, economic and industrial cooperation, support for developing countries, environmental and conservation issues, science and technology promotion, and academic, cultural and youth exchange. The Declaration essentially upgraded the EC–Japan relationship by building a lofty platform from which to gaze down at trade conflicts in wider perspective. The success of such initiatives can only be judged in retrospect, but there is some evidence that the implementation of the Declaration has yielded concrete results.[48]

In seeking to strengthen EC–Japan relations, attention has been drawn to the disparity in market access between the EC and Japan. It is argued (on the European side) that, while the completion of the 1992 process has increased opportunities for the Japanese in Europe, the path to the Japanese

EC–Japan Business News 1994. The creation of the Single European Market
in 1992 has expanded the EC–Japan
dialogue.

market is strewn with technical and administrative import barriers and
structural obstacles inherent in the Japanese economic system.[49] Underlying cultural differences may account for differences in the mechanism
of trade, but the yawning chasm between Japan's exports to Europe and
Europe's exports to Japan has become the target of demands for positive
action. Jean-Pierre Leng, as EC Ambassador to Japan, expressed the mood
of Europe in this regard:

> it is important to understand that Japan will be judged not by
> the number of plans, programs and studies which it launches,
> or even by the number of reforms it introduces. It will be
> judged by the effect of these measures, by what EC Vice
> President Sir Leon Brittan has called the evidence of change,
> and here the latest trade figures make gloomy reading.[50]

A report by a high-level Japanese advisory committee submitted to the
Ministry of Foreign Affairs at the end of 1992 put forward the current
Japanese thinking on trade with Europe:

> It would not be an overstatement to say that the Japan–EC

> trade and investment imbalance stems to some extent from an
> imbalance of mutual interest . . . To increase EC exports to
> Japan, EC countries must urgently raise the level of European
> interest in Japan. . . . the image of the Japanese market being
> closed is, to a degree, a fixed concept in the EC.[51]

The report went on to urge:

> better Japanese access to the EC market, including abolishment
> of discriminatory quantitative restrictions against more than 40
> Japanese products as well as arbitrary anti-dumping measures
> and local content regulations.[52]

It is noticeable that approximately the same themes have surfaced repeatedly in the postwar trading history of Japan and Europe. The question of
balance is always a matter of perspective.

The Uruguay Round of multilateral trade negotiations was initiated
under the auspices of GATT in 1986 and was finally concluded amidst
much fanfare in 1993. Seen as the most ambitious set of trade negotiations
ever conducted, the Uruguay Round has encompassed all aspects of trade
and, in seeking solutions on the liberalization of markets, focused attention
on the global economic factors which inform the EC–Japan relationship.

In a sense, the conclusion of the Uruguay Round some three years past
the original deadline provides a *de facto* postscript on 'the road to 1992' and
the evolving relationship between Japan and the European Community. As
a comprehensive platform for free trade, it contextualized the 'liberalising,
deregulatory emphasis of the Single Market' and threw into sharp relief the
individual perspectives of the participating nations.[53]

The creation of the Single Market from 1 January 1993 has been a
spur to trade and has stimulated significant levels of Japanese foreign
direct investment into the European Community, particularly through
the bubble economy years of the 1980s. Recessionary forces have greatly
slowed the progress of new investment from Japan but the expansion of
existing projects and the increase in Japanese research and design facilities
are but two ways in which the Japanese continue to make their presence
in Europe felt.

The corporate entity of the European Community may dictate the
economic parameters of Japan's relationship with Europe but it remains
the individual member states who attract trade and investment and who
play host to the considerable numbers of Japanese who have come to live
and work in Europe. This is the human face of the EC–Japan relationship
which has its own dynamic in the lifestyles and experiences of the Japanese
away from home.

3   Living in Europe: Expectations and Experience

In Japan's relationship with the outside world, there is a long tradition of cultural assimilation and metamorphosis. Ever the nation of borrowers to some, she has selectively absorbed influences from abroad and eventually, like the butterfly emerging from its chrysalis, transformed them into something distinctively Japanese.

Borrowing from the West in the Meiji period (1868–1912) was systematically and effectively accomplished in aid of Japan's rapid industrialization. If the technology was western, however, the values were determinedly Japanese.

The postwar period again saw Japan fixing her gaze upon the West and particularly America, seeking the know-how which would sustain her recovery and fuel her economic growth. The Occupation authorities may have brought the trappings of American culture to Japan but her underbelly remained unquestionably Japanese.

Japan's encounters with Europe have similarly been characterized by curiosity and a desire to learn if not adapt to European ways. In recent years, trade and inward investment have thrown the EC–Japan relationship into high relief. As the Japanese presence in Europe has accordingly increased under the banner of internationalization, considerations of economic interest have become tied to aspects of cultural interchange. How the Japanese live in Europe and whether a tradition of cultural assimilation and social integration are compatible forces has yet to be determined.

There is a Japanese community in Europe of businessmen,[1] diplomats, journalists, students and a variety of other groups, many of whom are accompanied by wives and children. In 1992, 128,400 Japanese residents were registered in EC countries alone,[2] with London, Paris, Düsseldorf and

Brussels boasting the largest concentrations of Japanese. What was, in the early postwar period, a relatively small coterie of bankers and traders settled in the comfortable confines of cosmopolitan capitals, has now grown and diversified along with the spread of manufacturing investment into a host of provincial towns.

For the corporate emigré, the image of Europe is a *mélange* of past and present, high and low culture, of people and things. It is northern and southern climes, eastern and western vistas and an assortment of incomprehensible languages and unfamiliar customs. Just as Japan has been resistant to dealings with the corporate entity of the EC, Europe in the Japanese mind presents a daunting spectrum of differentness.

The artist, Okakura Tenshin, wrote in 1887, after a country-by-country tour, of the disorientation which such diversity then inspired in the foreign visitor:

> All these countries have different systems; what is right in one
> country is wrong in the rest; religion, customs, morals – there is
> no common agreement on any of these. Europe is discussed in
> a general way, and this sounds splendid; the question remains,
> where in reality does what is called 'Europe' exist![3]

Travelling through and living in Europe has been an aspect of Japan's shared relationship with the West since the mid-nineteenth-century reopening to trade. The economic, political and cultural consequences of renewed contact included the progress westwards of Japanese government emissaries, businessmen, students and other adventurers in search of opportunity, knowledge and inspiration. In addition to the official missions and student sojourns of the Meiji years, Japanese emigration history offers up further precedents for the present-day experience of leaving one culture behind to become part of another.

While the contemporary business, student and tourist presence in Europe reflects the prosperity of Japan Inc., economic hardship was the backdrop against which the Japanese first emigrated abroad in search of employment. Between 1868 and 1941 some 776,000 Japanese left their home prefectures, many in south-western Japan, and set off for different parts of Central and South America, South East Asia, Oceania and North America through both government-sponsored and private schemes.[4] The descendents of those who worked on the coffee plantations of Brazil and the sugar cane fields of Hawaii still form significant strands within the local populations and have, through the generations, become integrated with and influenced aspects of native culture. The degree to which integration takes place within such adopted societies may be relative to age, gender and social standing as well as the particular circumstances of emigration and settlement overseas.

A tour of Europe means different things to the Japanese businessman and the ordinary traveller. The one comes to Europe not out of choice but through the designs of his company. There are some within this group who decide to stay. The long-term residents or *de facto* emigrants have usually opted for Europe over Japan in the course of a fixed-term posting and for personal reasons such as marriage to a European national or the desire to complete childrens' education abroad. By comparison, those who profess a preference for the values and lifestyle of an acquired homeland are more rare, though the phenomenon of 'going native' has many historical antecedents in the Japanese adaptation to European manners and customs.

At the opposite end of the spectrum to the long-term residents are the Japanese tourists who fleetingly and collectively pass through Europe, their picture-postcard expectations generally realized in the assemblage of people and places that the package tours provide. In the last ten years the number of Japanese visitors to Europe has virtually doubled and, in 1993, an estimated 1.2 million Japanese tourists made their way to the various countries of the European Community.[5] Young and single Japanese women increasingly embark upon the 'grand tour' as a premarital ritual. Honeymoon destinations accordingly follow the pattern of their previous travels and encompass visits to Paris along with one or two other cities.[6] France, Germany, the UK and Switzerland consistently attract the highest numbers of Japanese tourists. Each country has its own distinctive mystique and allure and the superficiality of the tourist experience tends to reinforce the fantasy image which distance and unfamiliarity have bred.

A more complex social phenomenon is that which the lure of the Single European Market has given rise to in the posting of company employees and their families overseas. The 1980s decade has witnessed a dramatic rise in the number of Japanese representative offices and subsidiaries in Europe, prompting a parallel despatch of key personnel to institute and implement company practices abroad. The managerial staff who spend an average of three to five years in Europe are often accompanied by families, though the age of the children and their current place in the education system is the ultimate determinant of who will stay and who will go. Postings for technical staff are generally of shorter duration and geared to specific tasks such as the installation of machinery or the training of local employees. Travelling without families, these *tanshin-funin* or 'bachelor-husbands' must learn to cope, in the process, with living in Europe and living alone.

Companies vary in their approach to postings abroad. The well-travelled staff of many Japanese banks and trading companies undergo specialized language training early in their careers and may well be fixed on a career track to Europe. Employees working in the overseas divisions of manufacturing companies can likewise find themselves acting as roving ambassadors for their firm's interests outside Japan. The corporate expansion of the 1970s and 80s has opened up the prospect of a posting in Europe for many managerial and production staff whose career plans might never have featured a period of living and working overseas. The impact of this experience and its long-term consequences have yet to be fully assessed, but the direct exposure to European lifestyles represents a new chapter in Japan's relationship with the outside world.

Japan's historical relationship with Europe was rooted in trade and Christianity. The distance between Japan and Europe which so many early travellers' accounts conveyed was not purely physical, however; it was a distance borne of a deep-seated view of foreigners as permanent outsiders and non-members of the inner circle that is still Japan.

The Japanese word for foreigner, *gaijin*, literally 'outside person', expresses the view of anyone who is not Japanese. Its overtly negative tone, appropriate to the title and period of James Clavell's last popular novel of Japan's nineteenth-century encounter with the West, has been tempered with age.[7] Now, slightly disparaging or dismissive, it suggests the 'us' and 'them' of Japanese life.

Both European and Japanese tales of past parlays relay a sense of Japan as a unique and exclusive culture in which close bonding exists across the various social groupings of family, village, school and company, the worlds within worlds where foreigners fear to tread. Japanese social behaviour distinguishes between the concepts of *honne*, showing one's true face within the inner circle, and *tatemae* or putting on a public face for the outside world. This latter dimension is the Japan to which most foreigners are privy and this explains the frustration which underlies the West's relationship with Japan. The culture of groupism has a significant bearing on Japan's attitudes towards foreigners as it does upon relationships within Japan.

In her much-quoted study, *Japanese Society*, the social anthropologist Nakane Chie contextualized the different Japanese codes of behaviour:

> The Japanese are often thought by foreigners to be very reserved. A more accurate description would be that Japanese on the whole are not sociable. This is partly because, once outside their immediate orbit, they are at a loss for appropriate forms of expression. They have not developed techniques for dealing with persons 'outside' because their lives are so tightly concentrated into their 'own' groups.[8]

The groupism of Japanese society is inculcated and manifest from an early age. In family life, school life and working life, peer group pressure encourages conformism and sensitivity to the feelings of others. Conversely, the word for individualism in Japanese, *kojinshugi.* is suggestive of 'selfishness'[9] in a society where, it is often said, 'The head that sticks up above the rest gets lopped off'.[10]

Conforming to the will of the group has its positive aspects in the sense of belonging or interdependence which membership of a club provides. Japanese society abounds in the insignia, both real and metaphorical, of group membership from the school uniform to the company badge to the Gucci scarf, all emblematic of affinities of experience and values which the wearers share. For Japanese brought up in Japan, there is a comfort associated with behaving in an expected way, of fitting in, which all such things symbolize and which the fixed rules of social etiquette reinforce. Japanese social life is rich in variations on the theme of responding in a predictable and appropriate way to a particular set of circumstances. Gift-giving. the conduct of business, socializing and language use all have their own codes and conventions which defy penetration from outside.

The comfort of conforming is offset, however, by the pressure to conform at all stages of one's life. To some extent, pre-school-age children and university students enjoy a temporary respite from the cares and confines of the socialization process in Japan. Upon graduation from school or university and taking up employment, however, the working environment becomes a new platform for group consciousness and responsibility.

Japan's lifetime employment system has created the basis for a corporate group ethos which extends and focuses the network of relationships that dominate adult life. Recruitment into a large company brings with it what Ezra Vogel has termed 'a many-layered overlapping labyrinth' of loyalties,[11] placing company before even family in the general scheme of things. For the employee, from the point of introducing himself onwards, the company comes first.

Hired at an early age and from the same educational background, recruits are reared in the culture of a particular company and cultivated as part of a team. Group spirit is reinforced through the interplay of work and social life and such single-status features of employment as the wearing of uniforms and the use of the same canteen by both management and workers alike. All are united in the pursuit of quality and the emphasis upon human relations and effective communication mechanisms ensures that everyone is pulling in the same direction. In-company training schemes further encourage identification with the organization and its methods and the seniority system of wage increases provides the ultimate motivation to remain.

The male Japanese company employee generally follows a familiar path up the career ladder. He will probably marry his 27-year-old bride when he is 29 years old. He and his new wife will honeymoon in Australia, Hawaii or Europe. They will most likely have two children early in their married life and he will work long hours in loyal support of his company and in the hopes of regular promotion throughout his career.

The posting in Europe must first be seen in the context of such career ambition. It is the status attached to a particular posting rather than its geographical setting as such which determines the response to an overseas move. London, Hamburg or Rennes are viewed not so much as points on the map but as European headquarters versus branch offices, major production centres versus minor subsidiaries. Whatever the location, the desirability of an overseas posting is measured with respect to its impact on future career.

The financial centre of London, with its preponderence of European headquarters, is seen by most Japanese as a prestige posting. Its further attraction, however, lies in the fact that England's mother tongue is also Japan's second language. In a perverse sense, living in Europe means not living in Japan with all the unfamiliarity, both socially and linguistically, which that implies. Beyond matters of personal ambition, therefore, an assignment in Europe raises issues of lifestyle and acculturation which the Japanese, largely unused to dealing with foreigners, have experience of only within the group culture of their own society. Nakane wrote in 1970, 'There is no alienation, loneliness or irritability comparable to that of the Japanese whose work takes him to a foreign country'.[12] While this observation has been muted by time and the growth of the Japanese presence overseas, the disorientation produced by even a temporary suspension from the Japanese group remains an aspect of being posted abroad.

The homogeneous nature of Japanese society is best conveyed with reference to statistics. Out of a population of 124 million, only 1.3 million non-Japanese live in Japan. European Community residents in Japan number about 20,000, and Japan's largest minority, the Koreans, despite generations of birthright in some cases, have only recently been given the right to carry Japanese passports. In the last ten years, guest workers from South East Asia, South America and the Middle East have superficially and temporarily added to Japan's cultural mix, yet the society remains racially distinct with intermarriage rare and suspicion of foreigners largely intact. As one author has suggested:

> They have no direct experience of foreigners in their lives, no
> imperative to think concretely about or be concerned about

13 Japanese and British workers at the Nissan plant in Sunderland. A posting to an English-speaking part of Europe is the most desirable option for the Japanese (Nissan Motor Manufacturing (UK) Ltd).

14 Yaohan Plaza, 'Europe's First Oriental Shopping Centre' opened in north London in 1993 (MCH).

15 Japanese families congregate at the *Asahiya Shoten* Bookshop in Yaohan Plaza (MCH).

16 For the Japanese residents of Europe, increased leisure time provides ample opportunity for golfing and shopping on the weekends (MCH).

17 Japanese restaurants in London have traditionally catered to a business clientele (MCH).

18 The variety of Japanese eating houses in London has expanded in recent years along with the student and tourist population from Japan (MCH).

19 Ambassador Chiba and Sir Hugh Cortazzi (centre) at the annual dinner of the Japan Society in London 1990 (Japan Information and Cultural Centre).

20 Japanese artists and tourists congregate at Montmartre in Paris (MCH).

21 Japanese restaurants and shops line the Rue Ste Anne in Paris (MCH).

22 and 23 The 80 per cent of Japanese visitors to Europe who pass through Paris are catered to by a range of tourist shops (MCH).

23

24 There are more than seventy Japanese restaurants in Paris catering to a Japanese and French clientele (MCH).

25 Daimaru France department store in the Centre Internationale de Paris at Porte Maillot (MCH).

26 Hasegawa Michio, President of Saint-Germain France (MCH).

27 Saint-Germain France on the Champs Elysées accommodates both French and Japanese tastes (MCH).

28 A Japanese bookshop in the centre of Paris (MCH).

29 The Hotel Nikko in Paris under the shadow of the Eiffel Tower (MCH).

30 Japanese residents peruse the noticeboard in the Paris *Nihonjinkai* headquarters (MCH).

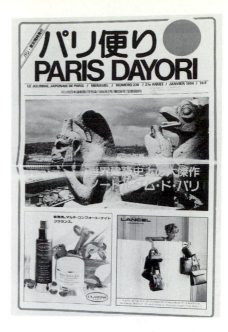

31 and 32 There are a variety of Japanese-language magazines and newsletters for the Japanese in France (MCH).

33 The Japanese School at Montigny-le-Bretonneux.

34 Learning about the Japanese postal system at a Japanese School in France (MCH).

35 The Japanese in France. A Japanese journal explores the lifestyle of the Japanese in Brittany.

36 Japanese students at Montigny take part in class exchange visits with local French schools (MCH).

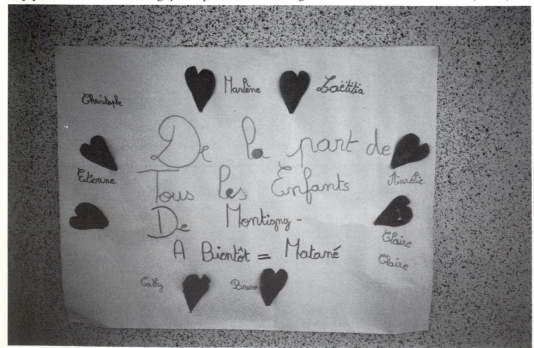

37 'Nippon on the Rhine'. The size of the Japanese community in Düsseldorf inspires press headlines.

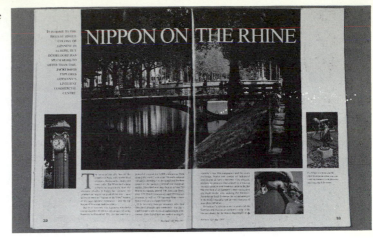

38 Immermannstrasse is at the heart of Düsseldorf's 'Japan Town' (MCH).

39 Japanese housewives shopping for groceries in Germany (MCH).

40 A Japanese foodshop in Frankfurt (MCH).

41 The 'Japanese' suburb of Oberkassel in Düsseldorf (MCH).

42 A music lesson at the Japanese International School in Düsseldorf (MCH).

43 The Japanese garden in Nordpark was donated by the Japanese companies in Düsseldorf (MCH).

44 and 45 'Huis ten Bosch', a Dutch-style resort complex in Japan.

46 The Eko Japanese Cultural Centre was built at Niederkassel in Düsseldorf in 1992 (MCH).

47 Amsterdam's Japanese community is centred in the leafy suburb of Amstelveen (MCH).

48 Japanese housewives chatting outside the King's Supermarket in Amstelveen (MCH).

9 A Japanese 'delicatessen' in Amsterdam (MCH).

0 Japan in Amsterdam. The iew from the Japanese estaurant in the Hotel Okura MCH).

1 Shopping for Japanese roceries in Amsterdam (MCH).

52 Passing a Japanese bookseller's in Düsseldorf (MCH).

53 JETRO's Iwai Yoshiyuki at the entrance to Brussel's Tagawa Hotel (MCH).

54 Export launch of Nissan Motor Iberica's *Mistral* to Japan, April 1994 (Nissan Motor Iberica).

55 and 56 The various types of Japanese restaurants in Barcelona attract both business and tourist customers (MCH).

57 A Spanish-style Japanese restaurant in Madrid (MCH).

58 Putting *kaizen* into practice at Nissan Motor Iberica, Barcelona (MCH).

59 Japanese students in Barcelona (MCH).

60 A Japanese *tempura* restaurant in Barcelona (MCH).

people living elsewhere. Foreigners therefore are rather like characters in a fairy story or a myth.[13]

Japan's insularity of outlook to some extent derives from her history and geographical position. A series of islands located off the east coast of the Asian continent, Japan has never been invaded by a foreign power and, despite substantial cultural borrowings from China and the West, has retained a sense of self and uniqueness which has distanced her both from East and West. There is a Japanese body of writing and thought known as *Nihonjinron*, literally 'discussions of the Japanese' which refers to the myriad of ways — linguistically, sociologically and philosophically — in which the Japanese see themselves as different in make-up from the rest of the world.[14] Variously adapted as the ultimate non-tariff barrier and excuse for cultural nationalism, Japan's sense of her own uniqueness has been alternately manifest in the periodic xenophobic outpourings of her politicians and dismissed by western observers as a self-generated myth. While not all Japanese subscribe to such extreme positions on their sense of national identity, expectations of living in Europe are inevitably tinged with reflections of these attitudes from home.

Knowledge of European lifestyles for the Japanese initiate may be based on previous business or tourist travel, collective company wisdom gained via the postings of colleagues, as well as the popular or media image of particular countries and people. Prior to a posting, mixed feelings of anticipation and concern are shared by company employees, their wives and children, who may respectively and simultaneously view three years in Paris as a struggle with the French language and communication in the workplace, a post-honeymoon return to the city of *haute couture* and *cuisine* and an educational challenge ending with returnee status in Japan.

Large companies generally provide programmes of pre-departure training for employees and their families going abroad. Language tuition and orientation briefings of varying length focus attention on the skills that will be needed to cope in a new environment. The ability of families to adapt successfully is seen as essential to the experience of working overseas. In firms such as Nissan Motor Deutschland, family life, language and education are addressed as the key priorities in planning for a posting overseas.[15]

Language and communication worries dominate the preparations of Japanese employees going to Europe and are the most frequently cited problem during the course of their stay. The study of English is compulsory in Japanese schools and most children will graduate with a minimum of six years of what is seen as an essential tool of corporate life. While methods of study emphasize grammar and reading and writing over conversational

ability, a grounding in these areas does form the basis for future improvement. Given this background, a posting to an English-speaking part of
Europe is the most desirable option for the Japanese.

In addition to Britain, business can readily be conducted in English in
the Netherlands, Belgium, Germany and other parts of northern Europe
and these countries inevitably attract considerable investment from Japan.
Despite the use of English in the workplace, communication between
Japanese and local staff through the medium of a second language
can compound communication problems arising from wider cultural
differences such as contrasting styles of decision-making. Few Europeans
working for the Japanese develop a serious proficiency in the Japanese
language and the tendency of many Japanese to engage in tangential and
incomprehensible conversations with colleagues in company meetings is
highlighted as a cause for resentment in all parts of Europe. While there
are some Japanese managers whose length of posting and commitment may
result in the development of French, German or Italian language skills, in
general a spirit of pragmatism prevails and English remains the language
through which the Japanese channel their efforts at communication.

Through schooling and experience, English has become the second
language of the Japanese. In terms of linguistic affinities, however, Spanish
is the European language – with its similarity of vowel sounds – which
many cite as the easiest for them to learn. The history of emigration
and investment into South America has created a core group of Japanese
Spanish-speakers within the international business community. It is not
surprising, therefore, that many companies transfer Spanish-speaking staff
between the two continents to serve their global strategic needs.

But communication is not merely a matter of linguistic competence.
The experience of Japanese companies in Europe repeatedly points to
the wider cultural differences which can fuel misunderstanding and
inhibit effective exchange. The indirectness of the Japanese language
and a corresponding understatement in body language does not always
translate well into other languages and a European setting. European
employees may complain that they are expected to understand unspoken
wishes and indirect commands and to be sensitive to the subtleties of
expression of Japanese bosses and colleagues. Conversely, communicating
through a second language can lead to directions or feelings being relayed
in an unintentionally blunt or offensive manner. For the Japanese operating
in a foreign environment, the negative response to such misinterpreted
behaviour can vary greatly between the British, the French and the
Germans, adding a further layer to the complexities of interpersonal
relations.

The factor of age also affects communication and the attitudes and language skills of the Japanese posted abroad. In the early days of Japanese foreign investment, older and more senior managers were sent to Europe to engage in the groundbreaking activities involved in establishing a presence and a network for future expansion. Along with the increasing localization of managerial roles, the company employees who take up posts in Japanese subsidiaries and offices across Europe are younger and more international in outlook. This affects employee relations and integration within host communities. Just as generational differences are influencing the changing values and lifestyles of Japan's own society, this society transplanted abroad will similarly vary in its perspectives.

The focus of human relations in Japan is harmony, achieving a state of equilibrium between individuals, groups and within society at large. The codes of behaviour which result in this harmonious interplay may be confused through contact with foreigners even in Japan. Outside Japan, as with a posting in Europe, the rule of law applies and all the certainties of life, along with familiar communication and behavioural mechanisms, break down. The traditional ambivalence of the Japanese towards foreigners, referred to by some as the 'gaijin complex',[16] derives from this uncertainty, this sense of being all at sea in an environment that is not Japan.

Japanese company employees working in Europe have immediate access to a new company group in the network that their position provides. Cultural adaptation is facilitated by the size of the company's presence in Europe and by that of the local Japanese community. Essentially, it is the job that they have been sent out to do that acts as a stabilizing force despite any linguistic and communication difficulties that may arise.

For Japanese company wives, however, their husband's posting to Europe necessitates a far more dramatic change of lifestyle. Many Japanese wives will accompany their husbands on a European posting, depending on the ages of children. In doing so, their usual role of managing the household and overseeing the childrens' education is structurally impaired by limited language skills and differences in cultures and customs. The affluent expatriate existence may hold its attractions for some, but the reality of coping with accommodation arrangements, medical care, banking, shopping, driving and other foreign systems in an unfamiliar language places a considerable burden on Japanese women who have been largely unused to contact with other cultures.

The dynamic between husbands and wives can alter as a result of a posting in Europe where men may adopt a more interdependent role in household affairs and liaison with schools, due to the foreign language deficiencies of their wives. Shorter working hours and an increase in holidays and leisure time also affects relationships between couples and within families who may have led far more separate existences in Japan but who now experience the benefits of the European rather than the Japanese lifestyle and pattern of work. The 'company comes first' mentality is gradually being eroded across the generations in Japan. A posting in Europe can also contribute a comparative perspective to working life and family life back home. The Japanese wife's standard definition of a good husband as one who is 'healthy and at work' may come to be redefined in the light of such experience.

Among the positive aspects of living in Europe, Japanese residents point to the freedom from social responsibilities and family ties which the distance from Japan allows. Caring for ageing parents and the constant need to smooth relationships with associates and neighbours is temporarily alleviated by a sojourn overseas. For many, a short-term posting in Europe is approached as an interlude in life's structured path, an extended holiday with built-in opportunities for travel, sightseeing and acquiring an ample supply of European luxury goods.

Japanese-style relationships are not completely left behind during a stay in Europe. Within the companies themselves and in the locally generated wives' groups, traditional hierarchies prevail. Women tend to identify themselves in relation to their husband's company and the opinion of the managing director's wife may still hold sway. For some, it must be said, such social tiering is less palatable in a foreign land.

The physical circumstances of living in Europe contrast markedly with those in Japan. In Japan, population density and overcrowding exacts its toll on the urban dweller who faces a lengthy commuting distance into work each day. Families, meanwhile, live in cramped accommodation with poor leisure facilities and limited access to parks and open spaces. In Europe, a better standard of housing and private gardens make for a lifestyle that many find less restricted and more relaxed. Opportunities for socializing and entertaining at home are enhanced by the quality of housing, increase in leisure time and shorter commuting distances.

The contrast in lifestyle between the major cities and the provinces is another aspect of European diversity to which the Japanese must adapt. Many preconceptions exist of the high culture of Europe, of the museums and monuments of which each capital can claim its fair share. For the Japanese, the antiquity of Europe is an attraction in itself which enriches their stay and motivates their travel across the borders of one country after another.

In coming to Britain, images of Buckingham Palace, the British Museum and the Tower of London may rise to the fore. But the reality for the Fujitsu employee posted to County Durham or the Toyota carworker posted to Derbyshire is far different and arguably permits a deeper penetration into British life. So it is across Europe, as the primarily urban Japanese expatriates have followed their companies to the capitals but also to the provinces where a further unknown culture prevails.

The different manners and customs of Europe hold a certain fascination for the Japanese. While access to Japanese food supplies is a staple requirement of living abroad, foreign cuisines and wines, as some of the more non-confrontational aspects of cultural acquisition, are readily sampled by most. Ordering in French or Spanish restaurants may require a certain linguistic competence and familiarity with local practice but this is all part of the veneer of Europeanization which the Japanese resident willingly adopts and re-exports in person back to Japan.

Japanese company wives generally do not work when accompanying their husbands on a posting abroad. Their leisure time is thus variously spent in pursuit of the knowledge, skills and experience of foreign culture. Far more Japanese women than men embark upon the study of European languages, drawing upon the facilities of established institutes and private tutors. Classes in the arts, crafts, cookery, music and dance also provide an entrée to the society in which they temporarily reside. Inhibitions over language ability initially restrict contact with European neighbours and colleagues but community-based organized activities act as a vehicle for interchange. Shopping may be done in the company of Japanese friends, but this universal pastime again demands a certain familiarity with local culture and vernacular expression.

The discipline and control inherent in Japanese society is not mirrored in European life and this can be seen as a negative point of comparison for the Japanese abroad. On an escalating scale of social irresponsibility, litter, graffiti and crime confront the Japanese with ingrained differences in the outlook and structure of European societies. Some have directly experienced car thefts, burglaries and muggings, prompting efforts on the part of companies and embassies to brief new arrivals on the perils of living in a less-regulated and group-oriented culture and to encourage caution in the overt display of the spoils of Japan's economic success.

To what extent the Japanese in Europe are the target of racial prejudice is more difficult to ascertain. Individual incidents have occurred and the legacy of the Second World War continues to spark resentment through the generations. The more international milieus of London, Paris and Brussels mitigate against such hostility. In both the cities and the provinces, however, a blend of distance and ignorance can rebound upon relations with Japanese residents whose affluence may be associated with trade frictions and an imbalance of industrial success. While not dominant factors in the Japanese experience of Europe, instances of crime and prejudice do represent the downside of living outside Japan.

Japan's education system accounts in some significant measure for the reinforcement of group behaviour in society. What is, by western standards, a highly competitive and, in some views, uncreative series of hurdles to be leaped over in consecutive stages, is for the Japanese an egalitarian and yet meritocratic channelling device in which success is determined by the ability to absorb and reproduce factual knowledge and to emerge through the socialization process of schooling as a lifelong member of the Japanese group. Six years of compulsory primary education (ages 6–12) are followed by three years of junior high (ages 12–15). As many as 94 per cent of Japanese then go on to senior high school (ages 15–18) and approximately one-third to university or some form of higher education. The 'examination hell' that marks entry into each phase of the system is a rigorous rite of passage that ideally culminates in entry to a chosen university, ensuring a particular career and recruitment by a mainstream company. This at least was the Japanese dream until the bursting of the bubble economy began to undermine recruitment prospects and the predictable career pattern.

The education system has certainly been the key to Japan's success. A highly centralized curriculum results in a nation of graduates who are educated in the same core body of knowledge. Combined with the group ethic which moulds the patterns of Japanese life, schooling in Japan produces a mobilizable and cooperative workforce which is trained in the principles of teamwork and organizational loyalty from an early age.

In *How the Japanese Learn to Work*, Ronald Dore and Mari Sako point to the relevance of such training to later life:

> It prepares people not only to accept as natural, but also to get comfort from, the patterns of co-operative effort, constant consultation, group responsibility and group sharing in achievement which serve to contribute to the efficiency of Japanese enterprises and to sustain their character as 'learning organisms'.[17]

Group responsibility is inculcated in students in a variety of ways, such as the serving of school lunches and the cleaning of their own classrooms and playgrounds. An atmosphere of discipline and hard work pervades the classroom, where methods of rote-learning are preferred over analytical practice, in deference to size (usually over 40 children) and the ethos of Confucian tradition.

The core curriculum is broad through the high school years and emphasizes the study of mathematics, Japanese language, English, social studies and general science. School days are long and augmented by Saturday morning classes. The lengthier school year further contributes to the intensity of the education experience which sees the quantity of classroom hours accumulated in twelve years of study matching that for which the British system takes fourteen.[18]

Standards of achievement, particularly in mathematics and science, are high by comparison with America and Europe, and children of all abilities across the curriculum are encouraged to do their best. Consequently there is no streaming, with the result that those in the lower half of the ability range do better than their western counterparts. The teacher's nurturing and rallying role is central to this process and the culture of groupism ensures that none get left behind. The system, as such, has been likened to a locomotive which draws along the entire train.

Parents, and especially mothers, play an active role in their children's education. The Parents Teachers' Association provides an organizational framework for involvement but the teachers themselves maintain regular contact with parents and ensure that the child's progress is monitored both at school and at home.

The competitiveness of the system and the high value that is placed on learning within Japanese society defines the mother's role as impresario in the overseeing of her children's education. The expression, *kyoiku mama*, or 'education mother' conveys the seriousness of purpose which is attached to her pressing, cajoling and encouragement of the efforts of her offspring.

Many Japanese children attend *juku* or cramming school to ensure that, after normal school hours and on weekends, they can have further opportunities to improve examination techniques as the next hurdle of educational achievement approaches. From junior high school onwards the pressure mounts and takes its toll on the lifestyles of children and families, who may question its methods but cannot afford to ignore its results.

The study of Europe during the compulsory years of education (ages 6–15) falls within the social studies syllabus. At primary level, students learn about their home environment first, and only in the sixth and final year begin to address that of the wider world. Senior high school students select social studies subject options from a choice of Japanese history, world history and geography. In the area of geography such study is perhaps more factually based, whereas world history arguably allows for more interpretive analysis of facts. Some emphasis is placed upon the Meiji period (1868–1912) and Japan's extensive borrowings

Origin	1989	1990	1991	1992	1993
United States	1,034	1,159	1,440	1,578	1,754
United Kingdom	364	389	483	590	675
Australia	134	132	128	168	196
New Zealand	42	67	124	159	189
Canada	276	350	470	560	629
Ireland	36	41	43	41	54
France	5	4	6	7	7
Germany	3	4	5	5	4
Total	1,894	2,146	2,699	3,108	3,508

Numbers of assistant language teachers sent to Japan with the JET programme (Monbusho).

from the West. A more contentious perspective on Japan's international relationships is centred, however, in the treatment of the Second World War in history textbooks and particularly the anodyne interpretation of Japan's aggression in China and South East Asia and the 'massacre of Nanking'. Both within and outside of Japan, voices of protest have been raised against the nationalistic and inaccurate representation of events, with the result that social studies textbooks to be introduced from the spring of 1995 will reflect some change.

Foreign language study contributes to an international view, and it is significant that English remains the only compulsory foreign language in Japanese schools, though French and German are available as additional subjects. English is studied by all Japanese children from junior high school age. As a high proportion go on to senior high school and university or some form of advanced study, most Japanese acquire a wide vocabulary and a sound grammatical base. It has been previously noted that the methods of language study result in limited conversational ability, and Japanese teachers are themselves deficient in this respect.

As Japan's push to internationalize has gained force, various schemes have been launched to improve the ability of Japanese teachers of English, but also to bring native teachers of English into Japan. In 1987 the Japanese Education Ministry launched the Japan Education and Teaching Program (JET) which has brought ever-increasing numbers of foreign language assistants on fixed contracts into Japanese schools. With the aim of improving the spoken communication skills of secondary school students, direct contact has been arranged with teaching assistants from North America, Australia, New Zealand and Europe who are providing tuition not only in English but in French and German. In 1994, a total of 4,179 JET participants set forth for Japan, compared with only 848 in 1987, acknowledgement of Japan's

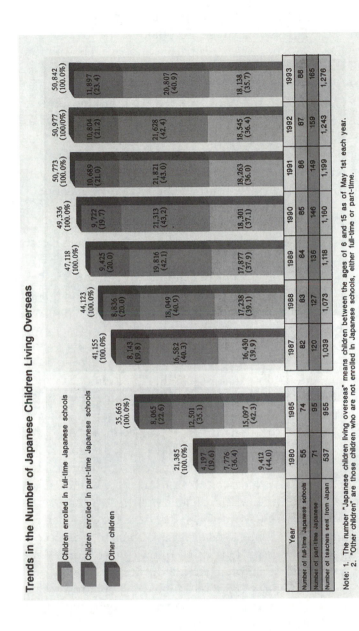

Trends in the Number of Japanese Children Living Overseas

- Children enrolled in full-time Japanese schools
- Children enrolled in part-time Japanese schools
- Other children

Year	1980	1985	1987	1988	1989	1990	1991	1992	1993
Number of full-time Japanese schools	55	74	82	83	84	85	86	87	88
Number of part-time Japanese	71	95	120	127	136	146	149	159	165
Number of teachers sent from Japan	537	955	1,039	1,073	1,118	1,160	1,199	1,243	1,276

Totals (100.0%): 1980: 21,385; 1985: 35,663; 1987: 41,155; 1988: 44,123; 1989: 47,118; 1990: 49,336; 1991: 50,773; 1992: 50,977; 1993: 50,842

Children enrolled in full-time Japanese schools: 1980: 4,197 (19.6); 1985: 8,065 (22.6); 1987: 8,143 (19.8); 1988: 8,836 (20.0); 1989: 9,425 (20.0); 1990: 9,712 (19.7); 1991: 10,689 (21.0); 1992: 10,804 (21.2); 1993: 11,897 (23.4)

Children enrolled in part-time Japanese schools: 1980: 7,776 (36.4); 1985: 12,501 (35.1); 1987: 16,582 (40.3); 1988: 18,049 (40.9); 1989: 19,816 (42.1); 1990: 21,313 (43.2); 1991: 21,821 (43.0); 1992: 21,628 (42.4); 1993: 20,807 (40.9)

Other children: 1980: 9,412 (44.0); 1985: 15,097 (42.3); 1987: 16,430 (39.9); 1988: 17,238 (39.1); 1989: 17,877 (37.9); 1990: 18,301 (37.1); 1991: 18,263 (36.0); 1992: 18,545 (36.4); 1993: 18,138 (35.7)

Note: 1. The number "Japanese children living overseas" means children between the ages of 6 and 15 as of May 1st each year.
2. "Other children" are those children who are not enrolled in Japanese schools, either full-time or part-time.

Trends in the number of Japanese children living overseas (Monbusho).

increasing awareness of the need to heighten her international profile.[19]

The importance of education to future career prospects is a recognized
fact of Japanese life. For the Japanese corporate exile overseas, then,
educational damage limitation is a primary concern. The uniformity
of the education system and its precise fit with Japan's homogeneous
culture make the diversity of overseas study an incompatible force in life's
otherwise predictable pattern. In her pioneering book on this subject, *The
Japanese Overseas: Can They Go Home Again?*, Merry White points to the
sameness of the system throughout Japan:

> That on a given day all third-graders in Japan are working at
> the same level in arithmetic, that teachers expect children to
> follow regular and predictable routines of classroom behaviour,
> and that the twice-yearly sports day follows a single sequence
> of events.[20]

These are cited as evidence of an educational uniformity which cannot be
echoed abroad.

There are, ironically, elements of cross-cultural envy in the West's view
of Japan's results-oriented system as a superior model while Japanese
parents and educationalists decry the drawbacks of their pressure-ridden
and non-innovative methods of study. Faced with a choice, however,
many Japanese abroad will opt for Japanese-style schooling for their
children.

The educational options for Japanese families posted to Europe vary
according to the countries and the areas where people live. Full-time
Japanese schools represent the safest choice and closely duplicate the
curriculum of Ministry of Education-run schools in Japan with the addition
of relevant language study. The majority of these are found in developing
countries though, in 1993, out of 12,853 Japanese children resident in
Europe, 33.8 per cent were enrolled in full-time Japanese schools of which
there are currently 32.[21] Of the other available options, 45 supplementary
Japanese schools which provide Saturday classes attracted 33.4 per cent of
Japanese children in Europe, while local or international schools accounted
for the remaining 32.8 per cent. This is in contrast with North America
where only 3.7 per cent of children attend full-time schools and 74.2
per cent Japanese supplementary schools. Language problems outside the
English-speaking world thus seem to force a greater dependence upon the
Japanese system duplicated overseas.

In recent years much attention has been focused upon the so-called
kikokushijo mondai or 'the returnee children problem'.[22] The rhetoric of
internationalization does not always match the reception which greets

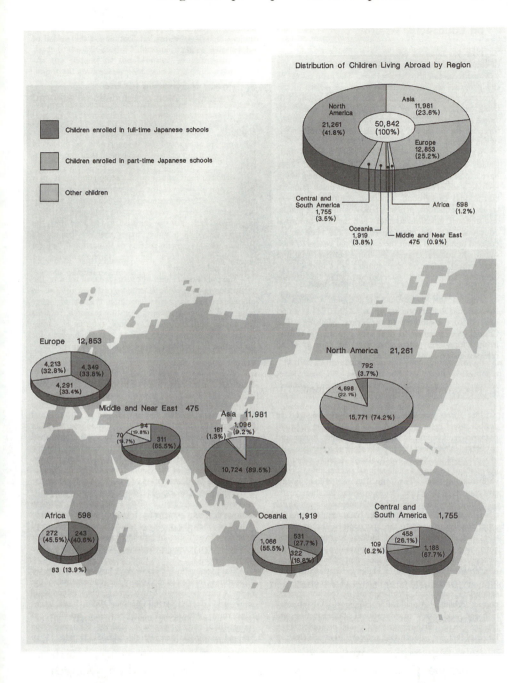

School attendance by Japanese children living abroad by region (1993) (Monbusho).

'It's My Turn' Publicity for Oizumi
Senior High School, the first state
school for returnee children in Japan
(opened in 1964).

Japanese schoolchildren educated abroad upon their return to Japan. Deficiencies in Japanese language or mathematics skills conversely combined with a mastery of English and other languages far exceeding that of Japanese teachers, makes such children stand out as different from the rest. Teased as *hen-japa* or 'strange Japanese' by their classmates, isolation from the group and even bullying may result from the open display of foreign-acquired traits. It is not uncommon for returnee children to disguise their language skills and to consciously ape the poor accents of their peers along with subsuming other aspects of their European or American veneer.

This problem does not just confine itself to the children of businessmen returning from a posting overseas. For their fathers, reintegration into company life can contain other pitfalls. Many comment upon negative reactions to their more outspoken behaviour following an overseas posting. A tendency to question the system and even more relaxed body language can identify them as not quite Japanese. For one Japanese businessman returning from five years in Düsseldorf, the dilemma was succinctly described: 'It takes three days', he said, 'to adjust once again to being back in Japan and four days to become a proper Japanese.' This notion of being 'a proper Japanese' is central to an understanding of how the Japanese live in Europe and also what adjustments must be made upon their return to Japan.

To some extent, where and what role they return to determines the ease or difficulty of re-entry. Japan's main urban centres – particularly Tokyo and Osaka – boast increasing provision of special schools and classes for returnee children. Studying among others with a similar experience makes the transition a far less traumatic one. Oizumi Senior High School, the first state school for *kikokushijo* was opened in 1964 and is populated with the alumni of American, British and international schools abroad. They seem more knowing than their untravelled Japanese counterparts and more relaxed with themselves and their place in the world. Oizumi is a special case, of course, and like the *kikokushijo* themselves represents the privileged position of some returnees who fit into Japan's more recently defined internationalist groups, those who may in fact have a greater voice in the country's future. As Roger Goodman has described them in his in-depth study of this subject, *Japan's International Youth': The Emergence of a New Class of Schoolchildren*: 'They are going to the top universities, they are being preferentially employed, they are proclaiming their "otherness"'.[23] In this sense, 'the head that sticks up above the rest' is setting a new level in Japanese society and filling a need for wider international experience.

Japanese company wives, whatever their point of re-embarkation, provide a further litmus test of Japanese society's ability to reabsorb those exposed to foreign ways. It is they who must adjust to a new overseas environment without the anchors of work or school, and it is they who must, on returning to Japan, act as the family anchor while readjusting themselves to former roles. Supporting schoolchildren through the returnee phase must be a high priority for the once-more *kyoiku mama* as well as smoothing the transition for a husband readapting to working life in Japan.[24] The nature of her own overseas experience will also affect the Japanese wife's feelings on being back home. Lifestyle, family relationships and even dress may well have altered through an extended stay in France, Britain or Spain. On returning to Japan, the layers of Europeanization are either gradually stripped away or retained along with a certain outsider status. The isolation of overseas life can thus be echoed back in Japan.

Reverse culture shock is a phenomenon which affects all emigrants on their return from whence they came. Orientation and reorientation are flip sides of the coin of cultural assimilation and what was once automatic may have to be relearned. The Japanese families who move and move again in pursuit of corporate business face, on the other hand, an ongoing series of assaults on their cultural consciousness ending for some with permanent relocation overseas. One long-term Japanese resident of Brussels, describing the stages of Japanese integration into European life, was quick to point out that those who totally adapt simply do not go home.

The majority do go home, however, and, for them, the experience of Europe may merely leave pleasurable resonances of an extended holiday abroad. It may also have its long-term consequences in providing another perspective on life in Japan. The accumulating numbers of Japanese businessmen and their families who have lived overseas add up to an overturning of images and a growing force in Japanese society which can question and challenge the European stereotypes and xenophobia of more inward-looking colleagues, neighbours and school friends.

For many, the career posting in Europe may be a one-off occurrence with its positive and negative aspects. As time and distance blur the edges of memory, however, those who went look back fondly on a period of relative freedom from the confines of being 'a proper Japanese'. It is not unusual for colleagues and families with an overseas bond to meet periodically in Japan to revive the memories of days gone by and to contrast present circumstances with their lifestyle elsewhere. There is, however, an inherent contradiction in the Japanese sense of nostalgia for Europe, given that, ensconced in their enclaves abroad, integration into Spanish, French or German society may well have eluded them at the time.

The British colonialist experience offers some parallel for Japanese expatriate behaviour in Europe and elsewhere around the globe. There are those who go native, to be sure, or who effortlessly fit into an international milieu but, for many, living in Europe essentially means surrounding themselves with a Japanese infrastructure from food shops to schools to social clubs and synthesizing European culture with Japanese ways. Levels of interaction vary individually but the cocoon of support which the Japanese build around themselves in a European setting tends to reinforce the stereotype of the Japanese as perpetual tourists moving in groups from Paris to London and accumulating their snapshot views along the way.

4 The Japanese in Europe:
Autres Pays, Autres Moeurs

The press reportage of Japanese foreign direct investment delights in references to Tokyo-on-the-Thames, *sur-Seine* and *am-Rhein*, those satellites of Japan that have followed its citizens to London, Paris, Düsseldorf and other cities of Europe. For many Japanese overseas, familiarity breeds comfort and the group consciousness that governs life in Japan contributes to making a European experience bearable by ensuring that Japanese support systems are there to ease the way. While not all Japanese choose to live *à la Japonaise* abroad, the tendency to colonize particular areas and to buffer the lifestyle of Europe with home comforts from Japan is something of a national trait and one with its roots in patterns of indigenous behaviour.

Some of the main centres for Japanese investment also attract large numbers of Japanese tourists and students. The services may vary to accommodate a diverse community but the essential principle holds true – that, when in Rome, the Japanese need not do as the Romans do but can eat in Japanese restaurants, shop in Japanese shops, send their children to Japanese schools and socialize with each other in Japanese clubs. How this infrastructure has evolved and how it functions in different countries are worthy of analysis. Its comparability to the Little Italies or China Towns of other ethnic groups is questionable, for the Japanese faces of Europe uniquely reflect the values and economic strength of a business community enjoying the spoils of internationalization.

THE JAPANESE IN BRITAIN

There has been a Japanese community in London since the latter decades of the nineteenth century when students, diplomats and businessmen first gravitated to British shores. In June 1879 the Japanese trading company,

Mitsui & Co., established its London office. By 1884 there were 264 Japanese residents registered in Britain.[1] When London's Nippon Club was launched for the Japanese in 1882, the charter explained something of its ethos:

> London has absorbed the essence of civilization; and because of the mildness of the weather and the modesty of the British people no inconvenience is experienced in daily life. Some Japanese are, however, apt to feel lonely as language and customs are so different. Moreover, Japanese abroad have a common failing in admiring too much the civilization and customs of the countries where they live and tending to forget the glorious history of Japan, and consequently committing the mistake of bringing back dangerous thoughts to Japan. In order to avoid such unwelcome developments we wish to offer a place where friendship among Japanese is promoted through mutual discussions.[2]

Even in those early days of living in Britain, the tendency to respond collectively to the alienation of overseas experience was apparent.

The Bank of Tokyo was engaged in trade-related finance in London from the 1880s. Between 1920 and 1940, the Japanese banking presence increased with the establishment of London branches of Japan's three largest commercial institutions.[3] As shipping and trading links between Britain and Japan grew, so too did the size of the UK Japanese community which reached a prewar peak of 1,871 people by 1935. The larger proportion of these were in London but such cities and port towns as Glasgow, Newcastle-upon-Tyne, Middlesbrough, Cardiff, Liverpool and Swansea had attracted their own cross-sections of Japanese students, seamen, small businessmen and labourers over this same period. The Second World War dispersed some UK Japanese residents but, in its aftermath, Japanese commercial interests were reinstated in London and beyond.

The small and relatively self-contained Japanese community in Britain was given new life with the influx of Japanese investment into the UK in the 1970s and 80s. While the Japanese population was 13,400 in 1982, increased investment and wide-ranging business links brought that total to 54,415 by 1994 with some 38,000 Japanese nationals concentrated in the Greater London area.[4] Meanwhile, the number of Japanese manufacturing operations in Britain grew from 15 in January 1983 to 206 in January 1994, bringing larger groups of Japanese personnel and their families to all parts of the UK. The considerable investment made by the Japanese automobile industry in the UK has greatly contributed to this process. Nissan in

Sunderland, Toyota in Derbyshire and Honda at Swindon account for concentrations of Japanese in the regions.

Britain has attracted over 40 per cent of Japan's total direct investment into the European Community, investment that has been valued at more than £13 billion.[5] The popularity of Britain with Japanese investors has been attributed to a variety of factors, both strategic and cultural. Japan's former Ambassador to Britain, H.E. Kitamura Hiroshi, isolated these as follows:

> First there is the English language, the most accessible foreign language for most Japanese people. Secondly, there is the infrastructure reflecting Britain's status as an industrial nation of long-standing – particularly in the financial field, as symbolised by the City. The third factor is the availability of a high-quality, diligent and productive labour force at a relatively reasonable cost. Finally, there is the welcome shown by the British government as well as by local authorities and communities to Japanese inward investment.[6]

The Japan External Trade Organization (JETRO) has been conducting the *Survey of European Operations of Japanese Companies in the Manufacturing Sector* since 1983. The ninth survey, published in 1993, pointed to the importance of the Japanese as employers. Compared to other countries of Europe, larger employee numbers per firm have been recorded in Britain where some 70,000 jobs have been created through Japanese investment. The largest number of Japanese company affiliates in the electronic and electrical machinery and parts industry can be found in the UK which has also attracted the largest European share of Japanese investment in the textile, chemical, non-ferrous metals and metal products, and transport equipment and parts sectors. In addition to manufacturers, Britain is also home to 83 Japanese research and development (R&D) facilities out of a European total of 264.[7]

The history of Japanese manufacturing investment in the UK goes back to 1966 with the establishment of YKK Fasteners (UK) Ltd by Yoshida Kogyo KK at Runcorn in Cheshire. (YKK's overseas expansion of its zip fastener operations brought a series of manufacturing investments into various countries of Europe from 1964.) As part of its globalization programme, Sony Corp. set up the Bridgend factory of Sony (UK) Ltd in mid-Glamorgan in 1973. In 1974, NSK Bearings Europe Ltd established its ball-bearing plant at Peterlee in County Durham. These early investments marked out South Wales and North East England particularly as key areas for further Japanese attention. In the later 1970s and 80s, Japanese manufacturers spread their sphere of activity into Scotland, the East and

West Midlands, Derbyshire, Yorkshire and other UK regions. As Japanese investment broadened in scope, so too did the experience of Japanese employees in Britain and the need for a network of services to support their lifestyle abroad.

The British and the Japanese are quick to point to mutual affinities. Two island nations, the Royal and Imperial families, the importance of tradition and ritual, codes of politeness and formality and driving on the same side of the road are comparable aspects of each nation's identity which make the one feel relatively at ease with the other. Historic ties with Britain are enhanced by the Japanese love of Shakespeare and the English Romantic poets. The Globe Theatre was opened in Tokyo in 1988, providing a purpose-built platform for the performance of the Shakespearean repertoire in Japan. Meanwhile a host of Japanese societies devoted to the study of all things British – including the cult of tea – abound.

For the Japanese living in Britain, however, such parallels and interests are insignificant when faced with the realities of a different climate, different food and a different pace of life. The fine points of contrast can be measured in the practices of some Japanese company wives who have been known to rinse their hair in Evian water to combat the effects of the hard water of London. There are physical and there are mental accommodations to be made in adjusting to British life.

Ask about the weather or the trains and most Japanese in Britain will shake their heads and agree that both are exasperatingly unpredictable. 'Three climates in one day', one frustrated Japanese golfer was heard to remark on an alternately fine, wet and windy day in May. Another thwarted consumer found the British car showroom a cultural revelation: 'They did not seem to want to sell me a car', he said, after a particularly maddening exchange. In Japan the customer may be king but in Britain he or she may be at the mercy of undermotivated sales staff.

British cooking also comes in for some criticism. The best, most would agree, is of a very high standard. On average, however, the 'meat and two veg ' mentality finds little to recommend it among a people who delight in the artful and exquisite preparation and presentation of subtle culinary combinations.

There is similarly a perception gap with respect to British standards of dress. The tradition of high tailoring that gave rise to the term *seburo* – as in 'Savile Row' – for suit in Japanese, is contrasted with the 'scruffy' style of the average Briton. According to one Japanese company manager, 'Many people think all British people are gentlemen, living elegantly and always wearing smart clothes . . . (in fact) everybody wears old rags: there is no

The William Adams Association is one of a number of Anglo-Japanese societies in the UK.

elegance'.[8] While such views represent an extreme reaction to the attire of some elements of society, there is also a time-warped 'Professor Higgins' image of the British – stylish, well-mannered and articulate – which throws the average punk-rocker and the disciple of 'grunge' into high relief.

Beyond superficial appearances, however, the class system is often cited by the Japanese as a social barrier in adapting to British life. Given Japan's achievement-oriented ethos, the fixed determinants of status in a class-based society are seen as a stumbling block to progress. There is a fascination, on the one hand, with the lifestyle of the upper classes and the trappings of inherited wealth while, on the other hand, a suspicion of the inflexibility of a system which measures success by birthright rather than hard work. That said, the 'old boy network' has its very real equivalent in Japan.

Various of the Japanese magazines published in Britain highlight this interest in the nation's aristocratic heritage. The glossy cover of an early issue of *Quality Britain*, for example, featured the kings, queens and pawns of a chess game as a backdrop to a sequence of articles on 'The Britishness of the British', 'British Lifestyle' and 'Sounds of Britain'. Interspersed with advertisements for British luxury goods and Japanese services, this contemporary slice of British life can be purchased for £23 per copy at the Japanese bookshop in *Yaohan Plaza*, Europe's first 'Oriental Shopping Centre' on London's Edgware Road.

Catering to Japanese tourists and to a resident population paid in Japanese yen, such facilities and prices reflect the relative affluence of the Japanese in Britain. A 1994 survey by Japan's Economic Planning Agency recorded prices for consumer goods in Tokyo as 49 per cent higher than those in London, making *Quality Britain* affordable along with other British goods and Japanese support services available in the UK.

An increasing number of Japanese authors with first-hand experience have set out to deconstruct the so-called 'elegance industry' view of Britain as 'a nation of country cottages, beefeaters and gold'.[9] Akishima Yuriko's books have tackled such diverse subjects as British women (*Igirisu no Joseitachi*), the changing role of nannies (*Mary Poppins wa ikite iru*) and British television (*Announcer was naze kietano-ka*). Her 'wry' observations on the make-up of British society provide a counterbalance to the tourist image so prevalent in Japan. Toshiko Marks has similarly addressed themes related to British life and mutual perceptions in a series of studies written for the Japanese. 'Mature Country Britain, Childish Country Japan' (*Otona no kuni Igirisu to narikin no kuni Nippon*) and its sequel were based on direct comparisons. Perhaps the most famous book to emerge from this wave of Anglocentric thought was Hayashi Nozomu's 1986 collection of essays, *Igirisu wa Oishii* ('Britain is Delicious'), which described the British temperament and mores through the nation's eating habits. Hayashi set out to explain and contrast Britain's growing popularity in Japan with the disillusionment felt for a Japan–bashing United States.[10] It would seem from Hayashi's analysis that America, Japan's cultural role model from the postwar period, is being usurped by a Britain of 'unruffled' demeanour whose more 'gentlemanly' approach to trade and business inspires feelings of mutual trust. The recent boom in British taste in Japan can be set against the experience of those Japanese tourists and expatriates who have, for a time, come to Britain and measured the reality against the image.

Britain is home to the largest Japanese community in Europe and London boasts the largest concentration of Japanese of any European city. While the current Japanese population of Greater London has been calculated at 38,000, there are 26,000 Japanese residents in the metropolitan area alone. These figures include diplomatic staff and employees of all official organizations based in London, staff of Japanese banks and financial institutions, trading companies and a wide range of businesses and commercial organizations from shops, restaurants and clubs to travel agents and recruitment agencies. Outside of the business sector, there exists a further body of students, artists, writers and exchange visitors.

Japanese manufacturing investment, student exchange and other factors account for high numbers of Japanese living in Scotland, Wales, Northern Ireland and various English regions. There are, for example, approximately 1,271 Japanese residents in Wales, 764 in Scotland, and 847 in North East England.

The Japanese in London have settled in such areas as North Finchley, St John's Wood, Putney, Wimbledon, Richmond and Acton where specialist support services have eased the transition to British life. Beyond the capital, shops, restaurants and other facilities have followed the Japanese to their various provincial bases where a captive clientele pays the inflated prices dictated by lack of competition and demand. Japanese mail order and home and factory delivery services have extended such business operations to outlying districts and to areas with smaller numbers of Japanese residents.

In London, families with children may choose to live in close proximity to or within easy commuting distance of the full-time Japanese school at Acton. In other parts of the UK, however, the location of factories and the availablity of housing partly determine where people live. Companies vary in their policies on housing. The spreading of Japanese residents across the wider community is sometimes encouraged to avoid the creation of separate Japanese enclaves. When Nissan first invested in North East England, for example, many employees settled in Washington and Sunderland to be close to their place of work and Japanese colleagues. More recently, however, some have moved to the cities of Newcastle, Durham, and the surrounding villages. A similar situation prevails in South Wales, though there is recognition of the benefits to be gained from the support that living close to other families provides. According to one Japanese manager:

> There is a slight problem because now there are around 50 Japanese families, and they tend to establish Japanese communities. Japanese wives especially tend to stick together, and it might be better if they integrated more with the wider community. But they find it very comfortable to live here.[11]

Being 'comfortable' in Britain is not too difficult for the Japanese. They are warmly welcomed at an official level with liaison assistance provided by local authorities and various regional agencies. There is a British infrastructure which exists in aid of Japanese investment and includes cooperation with companies, education and training support and advice

Living in Europe. A Japanese-language
newsletter for the UK Japanese community.

from local police and medical authorities on aspects of crime prevention
and health care.

In addition to the help offered by host communities, the Japanese have
generated their own network of services to assist in the acclimatization
process. As elsewhere in Europe, the education of children is seen as a
key problem and one for which a variety of solutions have been found.
Some 10–20 per cent of Japanese children of school age in the UK attend
full-time Japanese institutions including the Japanese School in London
at Acton, Gyosei International School at Milton Keynes, Rikkyo School
at Guildford, Shi-Tennoji School at Cambridge and Teikyo School at
Slough. (Teikyo has also established a university 'campus' with its 'Lafcadio
Hearn Cultural Centre' on the grounds of the University of Durham.)

There are large numbers of Japanese children enrolled in state and
independent schools throughout the UK. In addition, eight Japanese
Saturday Schools have been established with Monbusho (Ministry of
Education) and local authority assistance. These provide supplementary
education and receive support from local Japanese companies. A total of
2,392 Japanese children currently attend the Japanese Saturday Schools
operating in Edinburgh, Telford, Cardiff, Leeds, Manchester, Sunderland,
Derby and London.

Through the 1980s and early 90s, the numbers of Japanese restaurants, food shops, retail establishments, travel agencies and business services organizations in the UK increased dramatically. Among these, the Japanese department store, Sogo, which opened in Piccadilly Circus in 1992, takes pride of place. Near by on Regent Street is Mitsukoshi which went into operation in 1979. Isetan joined the echelons of Bond Street's fashionable boutiques in 1988 while Takashimaya was established as a near neighbour in 1989.

Selling British and European products that cater to Japanese tastes and sizes, such outlets offer Japanese-style customer service in a British setting. The price differential is overlooked in aid of negotiating the purchase of a Burberry raincoat in Japanese or taking home a Peter Rabbit souvenir encased in perfectly-creased Japanese wrappings.

The previously mentioned Japanese shopping complex at Colindale in North London, Yaohan Plaza, opened for business in 1993. Its location attracts custom from residents and some intrepid tourists who can find a variety of specialist services under one roof. The large-scale supermarket and restaurants are complemented by a Japanese bookshop, opticians, hairdressers, and Sega Dome amusement arcade for children. The high cost of using such facilities is offset by the strength of the yen and the convenience factor, but Japanese residents nevertheless admit that expatriate salaries are necessary to finance this style of shopping.

There are some seventy Japanese restaurants in the UK, the majority of which are in London. Residents tend to describe most of these as 'for expense accounts only'. Japanese wives, meanwhile, have been heard to complain of the rarity of their visits to the élite Japanese restaurants of central London where their husbands frequently entertain and are entertained by business associates. The variety of Japanese eating houses in London has expanded in recent years, however, along with the student and tourist population from Japan and the growing British taste for Japanese food. Beyond London, Gateshead, Edinburgh, Manchester, Nottingham, Bristol, Cardiff and Bath feature Japanese restaurants that are frequented by both the Japanese and local communities.

The basic needs of the Japanese are well attended to by the shops, restaurants and service organizations from Japanese recruitment agencies to medical centres which can be found chiefly in London but in capsulized form elsewhere. While many of these sprang up during the 1980s as the bubble economy brought ever-larger numbers of Japanese into Britain, a long-standing infrastructure of Japanese facilities and networks pre-dated this great wave and readily adapted to a wider role.

A selection of specialist clubs and organizations provides a social focus

Japanese Satellite TV provides the Japanese in Europe with direct access to news and entertainment from home.

for the Japanese living in London and the UK regions. These include the Nippon Club for Japanese businessmen in London, the Scotland Nihonjinkai and Wales Nihonjinkai. Further groups exist for Japanese wives such as The Japanese Womens' Association in Great Britain (Eikoku Nihon Fujinkai) which issues a 'Survival Handbook' for residents. The Eikoku Bunka Centre provides Japanese women with a regular programme of lectures and visits to promote an understanding of British culture and society, while the more casual Oranges and Lemons Club similarly introduces Japanese wives to the museums and galleries of London.

A further range of Anglo-Japanese organizations operate as vehicles for bringing the British and the Japanese together. The Japan Society, based in London, was founded in 1891 to encourage the study and understanding of Japan in Britain. As such, it took the lead in promoting the Japan Festival 1991. Its sister organization in Tokyo, the Japan-British Society (formed in 1908), with its 'Elizabeth kai' ladies group and regional offshoots, performs an analagous role in Japan. Other UK societies which provide reciprocal activities for British and Japanese members include the Japan Society of Scotland, the North of England Anglo-Japanese Society, Eiwakai in Birmingham and Hashi no Kai and Miura Anjinkai (William Adams Association) in London.

The Japanese in Britain are additionally supported by a variety of information services. Japanese language newsletters are issued in different parts of the country for the benefit of the local community, tourists or members of particular clubs. These include *Living in Europe, London Dayori, Eikoku News Digest* and *Nichi-ei Times*. Japanese newspapers can be ordered on a daily basis; such is the demand that the *Asahi Shimbun* is now printed in London. For Japanese residents, access to Japanese satellite television ensures that the experience of living in Britain is not only comfortable but informed with news and entertainment from home. The English-speaking culture of Britain also offers the Japanese direct exposure to the British press, albeit to a society whose written heritage encapsulates both Shakespeare and the *Sun*.

The traditional Japanese affinity with Britain may exist in the realm of historical ties and abstract parallels. For the Japanese living in Britain, however, there is British culture and there is the culture of being Japanese in Britain. The experience of many lies somewhere between the two.

THE JAPANESE IN FRANCE

Since the nineteenth century, Japanese artists and students have found in Paris an antidote to the strict controls and Confucian heritage of living and learning in Japan. Many Japanese practitioners of Realist and Impressionist painting studied in Paris in the 1880s and 90s, adopting the uniform of bohemianism just as they gravitated to the Left Bank and Montmartre in search of artistic inspiration. Among the contemporary tourist throngs at Montmartre, there are still many Japanese to be seen drinking in the atmosphere and painting the portraits of their compatriots more briefly away from home.

Paris and other parts of France have attracted a large student and artist population from Japan since Meiji analysts of the West first acknowledged its creative magnetism. As a cultural mecca, France – more than any other country of Europe – has provided a base for such groups as well as Japanese designers and chefs seeking to penetrate the secrets of French *haute couture* and *cuisine*. There is a steady and related flow of tourist traffic from Japan to France which received some 820,000 Japanese visitors in 1993, and to Paris through which 80 per cent of those Japanese who visit Europe pass.[12]

The Japanese business presence in France similarly goes back more than 100 years. Mitsui & Co. established its first European office in Paris in 1878, following Japanese government participation in the third Exposition Universelle. Its purpose was to focus on business opportunities generated by the silk trade. While Mitsui Paris closed ten years later, the trading firm established its new headquarters in Lyons in 1923 and, in 1926, opened a branch office in Paris.[13]

After the Second World War, in 1947, Mitsui became the first Japanese trading company to return to France. Marubeni Corp. and Nichimen Corp. opened their Paris offices in 1963 while Sumitomo Corp. and others arrived in the mid-1970s. The Bank of Tokyo was the first Japanese bank to establish a Paris office in 1968.

The Japanese Chamber of Commerce and Industry (JCCI) in France was founded in 1963 to represent the interests of just thirty companies. By 1993 its ranks had swelled to 288.[14] The nature of the JCCI member organizations range from trading companies, department stores and distribution centres to tourism and transport companies, banks, securities and insurance firms, power companies and a variety of service-sector enterprises. In addition to these, the Japanese business presence in France encompasses manufacturing operations of which there were 121 recorded as of January 1994. Production facilities are largely concentrated in the food, chemicals and electrical and electronic component sectors.[15]

A surge of Japanese capital investment into France in the late 1980s resulted in a number of highly visible and controversial acquisitions by Japanese buyers.[16] Prestige office buildings, golf courses and vineyards, including *Chateau Lagrange* and *Chateau Lascaze*, were purchased by the Japanese. *Le Nouvel Économiste* and other arms of the French press have been particularly condemning of Japanese investment in such French institutions as the fashion house, Courrèges, the cognac establishment, Louis Royer, the élite Paris restaurant, Lucas-Carton, and the Carlton Hotel in Cannes. Japanese real estate investment peaked quantitatively and emotively with Nippon Life Insurance Company's plan to purchase almost a third share of the Forum des Halles shopping centre in the heart of Paris. As the bubble economy swelled prior to bursting, so too did the aspirations of Japan's Francophile business interests.

Over this same period, France attracted the second-largest number of Japanese manufacturing firms in Europe after the UK. The first of these to arrive was Canon Inc. which opened its photocopier machine factory at Rennes in Brittany in 1983. Another market leader to invest in a series of stages through the 1980s was Sony Corp. with its factories in Alsace and Aquitaine. Outside of Paris, these regions in particular have become associated with investment from Japan and are host to local Japanese business communities.

Unofficial estimates suggest that some 30,000 Japanese people are living in France today. A total of 18,289 are registered with the Japanese Embassy

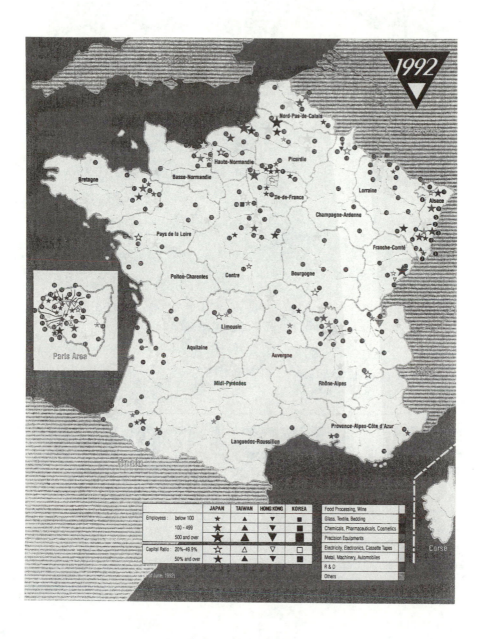

Location of Japanese manufacturers in France as of 1992 (DATAR).

Économie

COMMENT LES JAPONAIS VEULENT NOUS MANGER

Pour ouvrir de nouveaux débouchés à leurs produits, contourner les barrières, affirmer leur leadership économique, les entreprises japonaises investissent l'Europe. Les grands groupes financiers et industriels aidés par la haute technocratie nipponne ont mis en place un plan d'attaque dont la France est le point focal. Attention au choc !

Soixante dix huit restaurants, 18 560 immatriculés (dont quelque 1 500 artistes-peintres) repartis à peu près également entre Paris et la province, 90 usines représentant 61 sociétés dans des secteurs qui vont des fermetures à glissière aux cassettes vidéo, des fibres de carbone aux vignobles, des pneumatiques aux cosmétiques mais avec des effectifs moyens de 250 personnes, et une seule entreprise (Dunlop-Sumitomo) avec plus de

Le Nouveau Observateur highlights the strength of feeling about controversial Japanese investments in France.

in Paris and the Japanese Consular offices in Marseille and Strasbourg.[17] Of this number, only 7,157 represent businessmen and their families, the group which is, in fact, most likely to register with their embassy abroad. In view of such statistics, the overall proportion of Japanese business residents in France is considered to be relatively low in comparison with Britain where some 70 per cent of Japanese residents are from the business sector, or Germany with its high concentration of Japanese firms.

Paris has a well-developed infrastructure for Japanese residents (officially numbering 16,277) and short-term visitors. In the vicinity of the Avenue de l'Opera and the Rue Ste Anne, Japanese restaurants, *karaoke* bars, department stores, banks, shops and offices of every description reflect the needs and occupations of the city's Japanese population. There are more than seventy Japanese restaurants in Paris and these range widely in price and ambience given the diversity of their clientele, both Japanese and French.

Japanese foodstuffs can be purchased at some expense from such special-ist outlets as Daimaru France in the Centre Internationale de Paris at Porte Maillot. While Japanese food shops of this kind are generally patronized by business families, students and more economically minded residents satisfy their culinary needs in the less expensive shops of the Chinese quarter, around the Place d'Italie.

Japanese bakeries and patisseries such as Toraya, Yamazaki and Saint Germain vie with their French counterparts to attract custom through their own particular blend of delectation and presentation. Saint Germain France SA, for example, opened its premises on the Avenue Champs-Elysées in 1979. The Saint Germain chain, part of the Tokyu Group, already operated 150 outlets in Japan, integrated into department stores and selling French-style bakery products. Saint Germain's success in Japan inspired the opening of its 'pastries to Paris' enterprise in France.[18]

The thinking behind this venture is generally revealing of the Japanese service sector's attitude towards establishing a presence in Europe. The Champs-Elysées' Saint Germain was opened as an 'antenna shop' for the Japanese in Paris who account for 15 per cent of its clientele. Among these, 40 per cent are business families and the rest are students, teachers, artists and other customer groups. Native products like *anpan* (bread rolls filled with red bean paste) and *shokupan* (loaves of thickly-sliced spongy white bread) cater to Japanese tastes. Other products, however, offer more hybrid blends of East and West and have proved popular with Japanese and Europeans alike. The shop also serves as a training ground for staff from Japan who come to Paris on a regular basis and then re-export their skills back to Japan.

Japanese residents have their own department stores, art galleries, bookshops, dress shops, hairdressers and opticians. There are, in Paris and beyond, Japanese hotels, golf clubs, travel agencies, architects, lawyers and real estate agents, newspaper offices and public relations firms. The list is extensive and speaks of the needs of both residents and short-term visitors who seek to modify their experience of France with Japanese standards of service.

Many friendship and cultural organisations exist for the Japanese community. One of the most comprehensive in scope is the Association Amicale des Ressortissants Japonais en France, also known as the Paris Nihonjinkai. With its headquarters on the Champs-Elysées, it can claim an impressive 10,000 individual members, both Japanese and French and 3,700 family members.[19] Nihonjinkai has assumed a wide brief: to assist Japanese residents and visitors with all aspects of living in France and to provide French members with access to Japanese culture and contact with their French counterparts.

Nihonjinkai issues a twice-monthly Japanese newsletter, *Journal Japon*, one of the seven Japanese-language digests printed in Paris which contain a comprehensive blend of information about local Japanese services, news and cultural pastimes.[20] The Association has also published a *Japanese Living Guide to Paris*, listing the many activities and events that mark the Franco-Japanese calendar year. These include an annual bazaar, Art Club Exhibition, classes in Japanese and French, as well as calligraphy, *go*, *haiku* and sporting competitions.

The noticeboard in the Nihonjinkai headquarters acts as a magnet for Japanese people seeking practical advice on everything from French tuition to healthcare to travel. The broader base of the Parisian Japanese community is reflected in the atmosphere of the premises. Students, tourists and company families intermingle as they borrow books from the small Japanese lending library and pursue their various needs. The relaxed ambience is a far cry from that of equivalent organizations in the more exclusively business-centred Japanese communities of Europe.

Japanese business people live mainly in rented accommodation in the western suburbs of Paris and especially within the 15th and 16th arrondissements. The hierarchies inherent in Japanese society are reflected in the addresses of company employees. The presidents or *shacho* class gravitate to Neuilly; company directors to Passy near the OECD (Organization for Economic Co-operation and Development) headquarters; and less elevated Japanese citizens to the Left Bank and the general vicinity of the Hotel Nikko. These geographical lines of demarcation according to status are openly acknowledged with Rue du Chateaux

Journal Japon, the newsletter of the Paris *Nihonjinkai* (MCH).

in the Neuilly area jokingly nicknamed '*Shacho Dori*' or 'President's Street'.

There are Japanese living in various other areas in and around Paris but the bus route to the full-time Japanese School or Institut Culturel Franco-Japonais at Montigny-le-Bretonneux near Versailles essentially determines where families with children settle.[21] The Japanese School was first set up with 100 students at Trocadero in the centre of Paris in 1973 by the Japanese Chamber of Commerce and Industry. Serving a 6–15 years age range, it expanded rapidly in the 1980s and, in 1990, was moved to a purpose-built complex funded by the Japanese companies at Montigny. Enrolment reached its peak, along with Japanese investment, in 1991 when 500 students were registered at the school. The impact of the economic recession is reflected in the current reduced enrolment of only 380.

Teachers at the Japanese School have been sent by the Japanese Ministry of Education, and the fees paid by parents are similar to those charged by private schools in Japan. The School Committee consists of representatives from the Japanese companies in the Paris area who maintain an overseeing role. The curriculum, however, is set by the Ministry of Education and closely adheres to the native prototype for, as elsewhere in Europe, the purpose of such schools is to maintain a Japanese-style education abroad and to facilitate eventual re-entry into the Japanese system. At Montigny there are seven lessons per day as compared with the six offered by secondary schools in Japan, an adjustment which balances the quantity of coursework, given the lack of a Saturday morning programme in France.

In addition to providing a fundamental education, the Japanese School's philosophy is aimed at fostering international understanding. This is essentially pursued by establishing links with local French schools. Each of the nine grade levels participates in class exchange visits with neighbouring schools two or three times per year. For the Annual Sports Day and School Festival, the same schools are invited to take part in organized events. French is taught by both native and Japanese teachers for two to three hours per week as required by the local authority. A further form of language exchange has evolved with Saturday morning lessons in Japanese offered to the local community. Such efforts aside, the school at Montigny places its stress on cultivating and maintaining Japaneseness. While some Japanese children attend local schools for a proportion of their time in France, even the more internationally minded Japanese parents will transfer their offspring to the Japanese School for reorientation during the latter part of their stay.

There are various educational options for the estimated 2,000 Japanese

1 Madrid's Mitsukoshi department store stands on a prominent corner of the Gran Via (MCH).

2 Japanese honeymooners shopping for Spanish souvenirs in Mitsukoshi, Madrid (MCH).

3 Sogo department store opened its branch in Barcelona close to the Olympic village (MCH).

64 The Japanese garden at Clingendael, The Hague (MCH).

65 A Barcelona Japanese restaurant and *karaoke* bar (MCH).

66 The Japanese Pavilion at Expo '92, Seville.

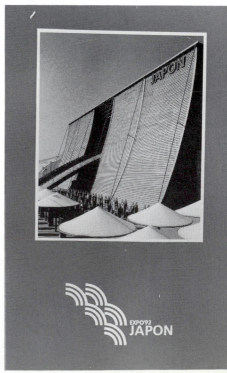

67 The Japan Festival 1991 *Hyde Park Matsuri*.

68 'Raw Fish and Wrestling'. Advance publicity for the Japan Festival 1991 in Britain (design by Iain Lanyon).

69 Alexander Wolfers meets Konishiki before the Grand Sumo Tournament at London's Royal Albert Hall (Tim Macmillan 1991).

70 Prince Charles is guided through the Japan Festival 'Visions of Japan' exhibition by Joe Earle of the V & A (Victoria & Albert Museum).

71 Sumo champion and Cumbrian wrestlers meet at Carlisle during a Japan Festival regional promotional tour (BNFL).

72 An exhibition of the work of the Japanese architect, Tadao Ando, in Madrid, May 1994 (MCH).

73 Japanese company wives introduce aspects of Japanese culture to British schoolchildren during the Japan Festival (BNFL).

74 Japan Weeks in the Netherlands. September–December 1991.

75 Poster advertising Sumo Festival, Düsseldorf, in June 1992 (MCH).

76 and 77 London's popular Japanese noodle bar, Wagamama, on
Streatham Street (MCH).

78 *Takarazuka*, the
all-female Japanese
review company at the
London Coliseum in
July 1994 (MCH).

9 Muji sells its Japanese 'no brand goods' on London's Carnaby Street (MCH).

80 Japanese shoppers congregate outside Fortnum & Mason in London (MCH).

81 The British Foreign Minister, Douglas Hurd, cutting the tape outside Daiwa Foundation Japan House in London, July 1994. On his immediate right are Lord Roll, Chairman of the Board of Trustees; H.E. Mr Hiroaki Fujii, Japanese Ambassador to the UK; and Mr Y. Chino, Honorary President of Daiwa Securities (Daiwa Anglo–Japanese Foundation).

修学旅行（イギリス）右端早津教頭先生

82 Japanese students on a tourist trip to London.

83 The Fortnum & Mason quality image attracts both Japanese residents and tourists.

84 Japanese tourists pause before the windows of Liberty & Co. on London's Regent Street during the summer sales (MCH).

children of school age in Paris and elsewhere in France. With eight buses collecting students from multiple pick-up points across Paris each day, the long journeying time to Montigny has proved off-putting to some. Families may alternatively seek exposure to local society for their children through a temporary French education. In such cases, attending Japanese Saturday Schools, of which the privately run Takehara School in Paris is but one example, provides a compromise to full-time Japanese education. Meanwhile at senior high school level, some students move on to the Lycée Seijo or Lycée Konan or to the International School of Paris; others enrol in the Japanese high schools in Alsace or Tours.

Japanese company employees and their families spend an average of three to five years in France which has implications for education patterns and inevitably impacts upon the educational choices made by parents. Japanese overseas schools are well aware of the difficulties some students may face in readapting to school life in Japan after a sojourn abroad. One teacher at Montigny noted that even though children may have attended the Japanese school during their stay in France, they are likely to be more outspoken and to react to situations with a French directness of expression on their return.[22] When asked to record their experiences of re-entry into the Japanese system, ex-Montigny returnee pupils perhaps predictably wrote of the 'boring' framework of lessons, poor pronunciation by non-native teachers of English and French, and instances of bullying.

The nature of the experience of living in France and views of the French vary across the business, student and artistic communities. Among the latter groups, there are many long-term residents who revel in the food, culture and less inhibited lifestyle. Some claim to have 'seen the light' and even share in Mme Cresson's criticisms of the workaholic culture of the Japanese.

If Japanese companies are sometimes branded as interlopers in France, the Japanese have their own stereotypes of the French to come to terms with. Loic Hennekinne, French Ambassador to Japan, pointed to these differing perspectives:

> Many French people are afraid that Japanese companies will conquer the European market, while many Japanese people have the image that France is a country of agriculture with a sophisticated culture, but not of industry.[23]

Within the business community, a further distinction is usually made between the pleasures of living in France and the frustrations of working there. Dr Ota Hiroaki, a Japanese psychologist resident in Paris, has addressed some of the cultural differences that confront the Japanese in France in his best-selling study, *Le Syndrome de Paris*.[24] Time and

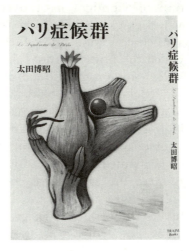

Le Syndrome de Paris, a study of
Japanese culture shock, by Dr Ota
Hiroaki.

again, Japanese restraint juxtaposed with French *élan* is seen to result in
an uncomfortable combination of disparate forces. The stresses faced daily
by the Japanese community have accordingly been monitored, catalogued
and given a name by this specialist doctor overseeing Japanese mental
welfare in France.

Japanese and French business encounters are often marked by such
clashes of outlook and style. Where the Japanese see themselves as seekers
after harmony and compromise, the French response to a conflict of
opinion is generally on a more volatile and argumentative level. One
Japanese businessman likened doing business with the French to learning to
adapt to driving on French 'rotaries': 'For Japanese drivers who are used to
waiting for signals to change, the French way of leaving it up to individual
drivers when to enter traffic is a difficult custom to master.'[25] Equally, the
degree of independent aggression required to enter into the fray of business
may be antithetical to the mores of Japanese social behaviour but, from the
French perspective, is an aspect of honest and direct dealing. Dismissing the
French as 'a nation of fast drivers and slow eaters', another Japanese resident
bemoaned the alien lifestyle and temperament of French society.

The Chairman of Sony France acknowledged some of these differences in a speech made in October 1992 on 'The Enterprise Culture of the Sony Group'.[26] He characterized the Japanese worker as more introverted and better at organising and planning than his French counterpart whom he described as more outgoing, spontaneous, creative and a better communicator. Different cultural positions when translated into the workplace were thus diplomatically viewed as complementary strengths. It is certainly true that the Japanese set some store by the quality of the French labour force and the rapport that has been achieved between the Japanese and the French on the factory floor if not in the board room.

Communication issues have been central to the Japanese experience of overseas investment. In Japanese companies in France, English is generally used in the workplace, though banks and trading companies in particular are increasingly providing foreign language training for long-term appointees. As for the French and their traditional disdain for non–French–speaking foreigners, this too is changing as young business people adapt to international business practice.

For the Japanese, living in Paris and living in France are not the same thing. Paris may engender the anonymity of all big cities and the associated problems of high living costs and crime but it is nevertheless Paris. Whatever the disadvantages, the lure of the French capital with all its cultural landmarks has remained undiminished in the Japanese psyche since the days when the French Impressionist painters first absorbed the lessons of Japanese prints. Japanese company wives particularly have the freedom to partake of the lifestyle of Paris, enrolling in French classes at the Alliance Francaise and engaging in sightseeing, shopping and other leisure pursuits.

Outside of Paris, in the various provinces where the Japanese have invested, other attractions can be found. Isolation can be offset by quality of life and the beauty of the countryside. Good weather and regional cuisine offer some further compensation for distance from the capital. There is a more limited Japanese infrastructure outside of Paris, but Japanese schools, food shops and other facilities eventually spring up wherever there are large concentrations of Japanese.

Settling in France entails a variety of adjustments and grappling with a host of unfamiliar domestic procedures. Apartments are usually rented unfurnished and Japanese residents, unused to operating in such a legalistic society, must learn to cope with the negotiation of contracts which affect so many routine aspects of daily life. Collective company wisdom is the well from which protected employees and their families can draw. For the individual Japanese resident without such affiliations, however, living in France can make for disorientation and loneliness.

The Japanese community in France has grown from the mutual business

interests which bind Japan and France together and from the long-held
fascination with which the Japanese regard French culture. The language
barrier and French protectionist rhetoric may be off-putting to some, but
the lifestyle of the Japanese in France would seem to balance the pleasures
of French style with the practicalities of Japanese home comforts. Between
the residents' and the tourists' experience there is a great divide, but the
Japanese in France share in a support system which allows them to sample
French culture in Japanese moderation.

THE JAPANESE IN GERMANY

A recent survey of the Japanese image of Germany produced an idiosyncratic
blend of responses.[27] References to Hitler, German beer, unification and
Beethoven suggested a diverse collage of historical and contemporary
sources just as the Japanese view of the German people as serious,
hardworking, inflexible and romantic drew on the stereotypes of German
militarism and romanticism.

Japan's early ties with Germany are centred in the legacy of the Meiji
period when the army, the constitution and the field of medicine came
under German influence. Like Britain and France, Germany tutored Japan
in these and other subjects through the years of modernization, and thus
permanently fixed her imprint upon the fabric of Japanese society. The
Japanese Ambassador to Germany, Murata Ryohei, has highlighted some
of the ongoing contributions of German culture to Japanese life:

> To this day German language literature by classic and contem-
> porary authors, i.e. Goethe, Heine, Mann, Hesse, Kafka on
> down to Günther Grass, are read by Japanese intellectuals,
> and German music, along with Austrian music, has become
> a permanent part of musical life in Japan.[28]

It is perhaps the heritage of German romanticism which dominates the
average Japanese person's image of Germany. However, it is an image
which is reinforced from within Japan. Replicas of historic German
buildings can be found in Tokyo, for example, and the Prinzchen
Garten ('Little Prince's Garden') complex near Shinagawa was built
with imported German materials including paving stone from the city of
Koblenz. Modelled after the picturesque village of Rothenburg, Prinzchen
Garten incorporates Käthe Wohlfart, a famous Christmas shop, which
caters to the Japanese fascination with another imported tradition from the
West. Referring to the 100,000 Japanese customers, mainly female, who
visited Prinzchen Garten between 1991 and 1992, Miyagi Yuki, President
of the Prince Hobby Corp. which conceived the complex, reflected upon
its popularity: 'I don't know why . . . but there are people, including

'*Guten Tag Deutschland*'. A Japanese-
language publication projects a romantic image of Germany.

me, who feel comfortable surrounded by a quaint and romantic German atmosphere.'[29]

Yet few Japanese ever meet Germans or have any concrete knowledge of German society or everyday life. A historian at the Deutsches Institut fur Japanstudien in Tokyo, Dr Gerhard Krebs, has described his own experience in this respect:

> When he told Japanese he was German . . . many would want
> to talk about Nietzsche or Kant, but (he) soon discovered they
> knew little more than the names. Other Japanese asked him if
> he carried his wife to bed every night.[30]

While the latter bizarre fancy may have been misappropriated from film culture, the conjuring up of such visions suggests, according to Krebs, the coexistence of two extreme images of Germany and the Germans in Japan: 'that of Hitler and the Nazis, and that of a romantic country with castles in the woods'.[31]

Japan and Germany became allies in 1936 but, in the aftermath of the Second World War, newsreel depictions of the atrocities committed by Hitler and the Nazis dominated the Japanese consciousness. The successful reconstruction and economic recovery of both countries has led to direct comparisons and sometimes unwelcome associations being made between the two. While such memories linger for some, the passage of time and the reunification of Germany in 1989 have helped to erode the purely wartime connections between Japan and Germany. Soon after the collapse of the Berlin Wall between East and West Germany, the Sony Corporation was looking to the future and investing in a prime site on the eastern side of the border. Not far away to the north of the Brandenburg Gate in East Berlin is the Mori Ogai Memorial, created in tribute to the famous Japanese novelist who studied medicine in Germany from 1884 to 1888. Japanese tourists today congregate in the vicinity to pay their respects and to purchase their souvenir pieces of Berlin Wall. Past and present are thus interwoven as the business of creating new images moves on.

Against the vague and impressionistic view of Germany, which many Japanese share, must be set the experience of those corporate travellers who have come to experience German life directly through a posting overseas. Japan's investment links with Germany have given rise to a sizeable Japanese community in Germany in the postwar period. Its disposition and make-up has been determined by the history and pattern of investment.

Japanese direct investment in West Germany began in 1955 with the establishment of sales subsidiaries by the Mitsubishi Corp. followed by Mitsui & Co.[32] By 1960 all of the leading Japanese trading companies had a presence in Germany and key personnel and some families had settled in different parts of the country. The Bank of Tokyo set up a branch in Hamburg in 1954 to deal with trade-related finance.[33] By the 1970s, a number of other Japanese banks had branches in both Hamburg and Düsseldorf and subsidiaries in Frankfurt.

The seaport of Hamburg was, from an early stage, an important trading base for Japanese companies, while Frankfurt's position as a leading financial centre attracted other Japanese business interests. By the mid-1960s, the city of Düsseldorf, in the German federal state of Nordrhein-Westfalen (NRW), was to become a strong magnet for Japanese manufacturers who sought licensing agreements with major German companies in the nearby heavy industry area of the Ruhr Valley.

All of the West German federal states, or *länder*, have actively pursued Japanese investment and established separate representation in Japan. The climate in Germany has been generally favourable towards the Japanese, despite periodic doubts cast by such influential journals as *Der Speigel* on the desirability of Japan's leading trading partner in Europe extending to her an unqualified invitation to manufacture within German borders. Certainly the experience of the main host regions for Japanese direct investment in

Rhein-Brücke, the German-Japanese magazine for Düsseldorf (MCH).

Germany – Nordrhein-Westfalen, Hesse and Bavaria – has been positive, though NRW has by far attracted the lion's share.[34] By 1989, as much as 51 per cent of all Japanese investment in Germany was centred in NRW along with a high percentage of the country's Japanese population.[35]

The majority of fully owned Japanese subsidiaries in Germany were set up in the 1980s. Between 1983 and 1994, the number of Japanese manufacturing investments increased from 20 to 106.[36] While the 1994 figure represents a drop from the previous year, Germany still ranks third in Europe after the UK and France in its share of Japanese manufacturing investment, and second in its attraction of Japanese R&D facilities which number 53. Electrical and electronics companies dominate the manufacturing field, followed by investment in the general machinery and chemicals sectors.[37] Over the years a number of joint ventures with leading German firms, such as the alliance between Mitsubishi and Daimler-Benz, have generated a range of successful working partnerships between the Japanese and the Germans.

Yoshida Kogyo KK was one of the first Japanese manufacturers to invest in Germany with its zip-fastener factory established at Mainhausen in the Frankfurt area in 1967. Canon Inc. set up a photostatic copier factory in Giessen in 1972. Sony-Wega Produktion later went into operation in the

Stuttgart area in 1975 to manufacture colour TVs. The 1980s then saw further investment in the NRW area by such leading firms as Fuji Photo Film, Mitsubishi Electric and Toshiba.

Nicknamed 'Little Tokyo-on-the-Rhine', Düsseldorf, the regional capital of Nordrhein-Westfalen, is today host to some 400 Japanese companies and has a Japanese population of 7,794 out of a total of 22,673 Japanese residents in Germany. After the trading companies' representatives, who arrived in the 1950s, came personnel from Japanese banks, insurance and transport companies and manufacturing firms. Meanwhile, the growing Japanese community gave rise to an assortment of shops, restaurants, hotels, *karaoke* bars, hairdressers, travel agents, Japanese lawyers, accountants, real estate agents, PR companies, and translation agencies.

The Japanese Club was established in 1964 in response to the increasing number of Japanese in Düsseldorf. The Japanese Chamber of Commerce and Industry (JCCI) followed in 1966 and the two have worked closely together ever since in support of Japanese industry and the local community.

While many similar facilities for the Japanese can be found in cities like London and Paris, the unique quality of Düsseldorf stems from the concentration of Japanese firms and services in a relatively small area of the city. Immermannstrasse, the tree-lined thoroughfare which runs north-west from the central railway station towards the city centre, is the heart of Düsseldorf's 'Japan Town'. Here stand the *Deutsche-Japanische Center*, home to the JCCI, the Hotel Nikko, and many Japanese offices, shops and restaurants.

The Japan Chamber of Commerce and Industry acts as a networking organization for the Japanese companies in Düsseldorf through its lecture and seminar series, Japanese language publications and liaison facilities. It may deal with its members' concerns about German labour legislation but equally supports cultural initiatives directed at the German-Japanese community.

Behind Immermannstrasse, on Marienstrasse, are the premises of the Japanese Club which caters to the social needs of those working near by. *Rhine No Naka Re*, a Japanese guide to living in Germany, was completed in 1990 by the Club. An ambitious three-volume project, it combines practical advice on living in Germany with a detailed analysis of German history, culture and society. An incorporated history of the Japanese in Germany reminds readers of the context in which this project was undertaken and of some of the stereotypes which residents brought with them from Japan.

To some extent language isolates the Japanese from the local community

Brochure of the Japanese International
School in Düsseldorf.

in Düsseldorf and elsewhere in Germany and makes for a selective
experience of German life. English is spoken in many Japanese companies,
and only a small percentage of Japanese move beyond a mastery of
survival German. Japanese wives may attend language classes at the
Goethe Institute but their husbands accept that being in Germany is a
temporary circumstance and learning German is a commitment most are
unwilling to make.

Four to five years is the average length of a posting in Germany and,
during that time, accompanying families may return to Japan in accordance
with the entry points in the Japanese schooling system. Germany thus has
its quota of Japanese 'bachelor-husbands' who must fend for themselves.
For those in Düsseldorf, the Japanese infrastructure provides some comfort.
Frankfurt similarly has a selection of Japanese shops and restaurants which
are much utilized by the local Japanese population. Elsewhere the Japanese
rely upon other cuisines or upon German food which most consider too
heavy and greasy for regular consumption.

The Japanese community in Düsseldorf is mainly centred in the suburb
of Oberkassel and has grown up around the Japanese International School.
The school's magnetic attraction for families with older children is such
that demand for housing in this part of the city is always high. The Japanese

have consequently been criticized by German residents for driving up the prices of rented accommodation in the locality. Oberkassel's desirability as an area in which to live is enhanced by the presence of a Japanese kindergarten which is similarly oversubscribed.

The Japanese International School in Düsseldorf provides an important facility for the children of company employees who rarely attend the local German schools. It offers primary and junior high school education and is one of three full-time Japanese schools in Germany, the others being in Hamburg and Frankfurt. Japanese senior high schools are located in Bremen and Saulgau.

Düsseldorf's Japanese School was founded in 1971 with funding from Japanese companies whose representatives make up its Board of Directors. It is the Japanese Ministry of Education, however, which supplies 80 per cent of the teaching staff. The school's enrolment figures speak of the success of Japanese industry in the area. It provided places for just 43 pupils in 1971 compared with more than 900 today.[38]

As is the pattern elsewhere, two hours of German tuition per week augment the standard Japanese curriculum which is spread over five days. A sister school arrangement with the Cecillien Gymnasium, and informal links with other German schools in Düsseldorf, lead to class exchanges and sporting competitions, undertaken in the spirit of internationalization. Outside of school hours, however, the concentration of the Japanese community in the district of the school makes for friendships mainly with other Japanese.

Such Japanese schools differ in their essential make-up from schools in Japan on which they are modelled. There is far less diversity in the student body, given the nature of the Japanese community in Düsseldorf and its business base. There is also a high mobility factor with students attending the school for an average of three to four years and some 40 per cent returning home each year. As in Japan, teachers focus upon preparation for passing high school entrance exams, but tend to encounter fewer motivation problems along the way among the cohesive and relatively élite expatriate student body.

The Japanese company presence is visibly stamped on the city of Düsseldorf. A Japanese garden was created in Nordpark in 1975 and donated to the city in gratitude for the provision of the site for the Japanese school. Another landmark, the Eko Japanese Cultural Centre is a Buddhist temple complex which was built in Niederkassel in 1992. The brainchild of Numata Yehan, founder of the Mitutoyo Corporation, it is aimed at fostering cultural exchange. German residents in the area viewed the construction of a Japanese temple in their midst with some suspicion,

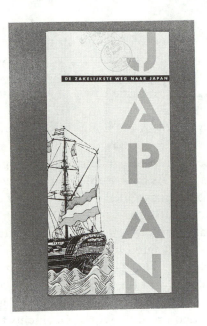

Publicity brochure for the Dutch and
Japanese Trade Federation.

though the opening of its cultural facilities to the wider public has, to
some extent, quelled such criticism. The Japanese in Düsseldorf have thus
superimposed their cultural presence on the existing face of business.

At an official level, the Japanese and the Germans would appear to
be making great strides. In March 1993 the German–Japanese Dialogue
Forum was instituted and a German–Japanese cooperation council is envis-
aged to facilitate technological exchange. Such diplomatic and goodwill
gestures have underlined the long-term commitment of the Japanese to
their involvements in Germany and of the Germans to their reciprocal
ties with Japan. On a more mundane people-to-people level, however,
exchange between the Japanese and the Germans – still separated by
differences of language, culture and taste – may prove a somewhat more
elusive goal.

THE JAPANESE IN THE NETHERLANDS
It was in the year 1600 that the Dutch ship, the *Liefde*, with its English pilot,
William Adams, was shipwrecked off the coast of Japan. The 400-year-old
legacy of Japan's trading links with the Netherlands is still remembered
there today.

Nagasaki Holland Village was opened in Sasebo in Nagasaki Prefecture in 1983 to celebrate the historical ties between Japan and the Netherlands and is visited by an average of 1.8 million people each year.[39] A theme park for enthusiasts of all things Dutch, it features museums of Dutch culture, replicas of old sailing ships and transplanted versions of the streets and historic buildings of the castle town of Willemstad and the port city of Hoorn.

In 1992, the *Huis ten Bosch* or 'home in the forest' resort was opened on the opposite side of Omura Bay. Its publicity literature promotes 'the tradition and culture of Europe', selling the development as 'a European resort with true comfort'. As the leisure boom proceeds apace in Japan, the Netherlands of old is taken as a lifestyle model and a cultural backdrop for European-style holiday pursuits.

Just as the artificial island of Deshima once provided a window-to-the-world for those who gravitated to the Dutch trading settlement during Japan's years of seclusion, Nagasaki Holland Village and *Huis ten Bosch* today offer a cultural platform for the sale of Dutch goods in Japan. More Dutch cheese is sold there than anywhere else in Japan, and a link with the University of Leiden provides work placements for Dutch students of Japanese who thus contribute to this flourishing trade.

Such portrayals of Dutch life may fuel Japanese views of Europe as a cultural museum, just as the annual tulip festivals held in Kaizu and Sakura focus attention on the most typical products of Dutch tradition. National image is an integral facet of trade relations and, while Dutch flowers, cheese and milk products dominate the export trade with Japan, it is high value-added manufactured goods from Japan that continue to contribute to the considerable Dutch–Japanese trade deficit.

As Britain's 'Priority Japan' export promotion campaign has given way to 'Action Japan' and 'Le Japon C'est Possible' has come to define France's more positive approach to trade, the Dutch government, in January 1994, launched 'Japan Trade Action' in a bid to boost and diversify its exports to Japan.

The Netherlands is the top European investor in Japan and ranks second in Europe after the UK in its share of Japanese foreign direct investment. By the end of 1993, as many as 390 Japanese firms were operating in the Netherlands, creating 19,500 jobs.[40] A number of these, including Canon and Nissan. have established their European headquarters in the Amsterdam area and 16 R&D facilities are contributing to technology exchange.

The central European location and infrastructure for international business partly explain the appeal of Holland to Japanese industry. Indeed, some 40 per cent of Japanese imports into Europe pass through the country

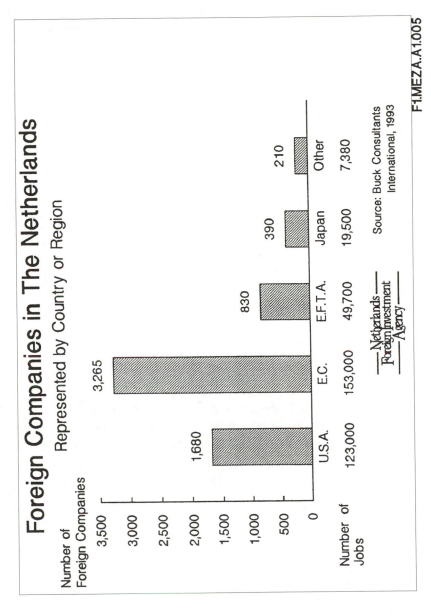

Chart showing numbers of foreign companies in the Netherlands (Netherlands Foreign Investment Agency).

and are handled by the Dutch.[41] Transport companies particularly have been drawn to the vicinity of Schipol Airport and approximately 65 per cent of the Japanese in the Netherlands can be found in the Amsterdam area.[42] Elsewhere in the country, the Japanese business community divides itself between Rotterdam, The Hague, Maastricht, Tilburg, Eindhoven and Utrecht.

In addition to its role as a financial and distribution centre, the Netherlands is increasingly attracting manufacturing investment from Japan. By 1994, a total of 45 Japanese manufacturers had established factories in different parts of the country with some concentration of activity in the chemicals sector.[43]

Yoshida Kogyo KK, the zip fastener firm, made the first of its series of early investments in Europe in the Netherlands in 1964. In 1982, Fuji Photo Film set up its colour film and prints production facility at Tilburg. More recent manufacturing investors have included the beverage producer, Yakult Honsha Co, and nappy (diaper) maker, Uni-Charm Corp. In 1995 NedCar (Netherlands Car BV), the joint venture between Mitsubishi Motors Corp., the Dutch Government and Sweden's Volvo Corp., in the southern Dutch city of Born, becomes the first mass production base for a Japanese carmaker in Europe outside of the UK.

There are currently 5,291 Japanese living in the Netherlands, of which some 70 per cent consist of company personnel and their families.[44] Japanese banks, trading companies and service organizations began arriving only from the 1970s. In those early years the majority of company employees lived in the centre of Amsterdam. Today, the leafy suburbs of Amstelveen and Buitenveldert, to the south of the city, are home to Amsterdam's Japanese and particularly those families with school-age children. The World Trade Centre at Strawinskylaan provides offices for a number of Japanese firms on this same side of the city and the Amsterdam Japanese School is just a ten-minute journey from Amstelveen.

Two full-time Japanese schools in Amsterdam and Rotterdam reflect the geographical spread of Japanese firms in the Netherlands. These are supplemented by five Japanese Saturday Schools located in Amsterdam, Rotterdam, Limburg, Maastricht, and The Hague. Maastricht is also the base for the privately owned Teikyo Junior College and the Teikyo Medical Centre, one of the few such facilities for the Japanese in Europe.

The Japanese Chamber of Commerce and Industry (JCCI) in the Netherlands is active in the promotion of economic and cultural relations between the Japanese and Dutch business communities.[45] The coordination of lectures, seminars and social events as well as support for the Japanese schools fall within its remit. These activities are highlighted

Newsletter of the Japanese Chamber
of Commerce in the Netherlands.

in *Kawaraban*, the JCCI's bi-monthly Japanese-language bulletin. The
Chamber also publishes *Benrichou*, a Japanese Living Guide for Holland.

The European *Go* Cultural Centre at Amstelveen serves as the venue
for various programmes organized by and for the Japanese community. A
Japanese women's club operating under the auspices of the JCCI regularly
meets there. Another women's group, Holland Kai, was set up ten years
ago to bring the Dutch and the Japanese together. This it successfully
continues to do. In the vicinity of the European *Go* Cultural Centre,
the Japanese women of Amstelveen can be regularly seen shopping at
the Japanese food outlet in King's Supermarket, collecting their children
from school, riding on the trams or cycling along the clean quiet streets
with young children in tow. It is a life different in style if not substance
from their lives back in Japan.

The Hotel Okura has long provided a meeting place for Japanese
businessmen in Amsterdam and, on the weekends, for their wives and
families. The Okura was opened in 1971 and was the first hotel of the
famous Japanese Okura Group to be established in Europe. Paris or London
would have been the more logical choice for this pioneering venture but
Noda Iwajiro, President of the Okura Group, hailed from Nagasaki and
chose Amsterdam over other European capitals in remembrance of Dutch

ties with his native city.[46] Today the hotel benefits from the approximately 100,000 Japanese tourists who visit Amsterdam each year but principally relies on the business generated by Japanese investment in the Netherlands. The JCCI holds its annual reception at the Hotel Okura and the regular rites of passage for the opening of new companies and the departure of Japanese dignitaries take place within its function rooms.

The basement shopping arcade of the Okura attracts business of a different sort. Here can be found a Japanese food shop and the only Japanese barbershop and bookshop in Amsterdam. Prior to the opening of the OCS Bookshop in the early 1980s, Japanese residents depended upon a mail order service from Düsseldorf for access to Japanese language books and periodicals. Today the communications network is more wide-ranging with daily Japanese newspapers and Japanese satellite television making Japan seem less far away.

Beyond the portals of the Okura, some fourteen Japanese restaurants and a small selection of food shops can be found in Amsterdam with a further eight restaurants located in the Hague, Rotterdam, Groningen, Maastricht and Den Bosch. There is an adequate but not extensive range of specialist facilities for the Japanese community in the Netherlands, a reflection of both its size and history.

Company personnel are posted to the Netherlands for an average of five years. Its central location in Europe and English-speaking environment inspires positive reactions among the Japanese. Certainly it is rare for Japanese residents in the Netherlands to attempt to learn Dutch; most will concentrate on improving their English skills during the course of their stay.

A posting in the Netherlands is regarded with equanimity by the Japanese. The lifestyle is good, with short commuting distances between office and home, and the standard of housing is a clear improvement upon Japan's urban dwellings. Most company employees can drive to work. For those who choose to do otherwise, the public transportation network is convenient and efficient. Leisure facilities are of a high standard and excellent golf courses exert the usual appeal.

On the negative side, Dutch service is considered poor by Japanese standards and the Dutch manner – in service and in industry – can be translated as brusque and pushy by the Japanese. A more serious problem is that of crime, particularly in Amsterdam. There, precautions must be taken against break-ins and car-thefts, partly fuelled by the drug culture which contributes so adversely to the city's image. To some extent the Japanese, in their protected suburbs, live at a distance from such harsh realities. Many will never experience crime in the course of a five-year stay. For others, living in the Netherlands combines cultural pastimes and a lifestyle of comfort and convenience with the threat of aggression and invasion of privacy that contrasts so strikingly with the crime-free society they have left behind.

On an official level, the Dutch have been most welcoming to Japanese investors. Internationally minded and conscious of the employment benefits which Japanese companies bring, there has been little incidence of Japan-bashing in the Netherlands. The Japanese, for their part, have been active sponsors of local cultural and sporting events and have thus played the role of good corporate citizens. The main concert hall in Amsterdam has been renovated by the JCCI and one Japanese sports sponsor actually carries a business card identifying him as 'foreign affairs advisor' to the Excelsior Soccer Club in Rotterdam.

Japan's celebrations of her links with the Dutch are set to peak in the year 2000 which will mark the 400th anniversary of trade. The Foundation of Four Centuries of Netherlands–Japan Relations is based in Leiden, home of the German physician, Philipp von Siebold, who so closely studied Japan and the Japanese in the nineteenth century. Here a vast array of Dutch–Japanese anniversary events will be coordinated. To what extent the historic image of the Dutch trading relationship with Japan will blend with present-day ambitions for economic partnership is yet to be seen. The millenium will serve to highlight, however, the passage of time and the changed circumstances of trade which once restricted the Dutch to an insular and controlled existence in the settlement of Deshima, and now find a Japanese community ensconced in the protected confines of the Dutch suburb of Amstelveen. Direct comparisons across the centuries have a limited validity, for those were the days when all foreigners were disparagingly described as '*bata kusai*' or 'smelling of butter' while, in today's world, the Japanese are engaged in a lively trade in dairy products with the Dutch.

THE JAPANESE IN BELGIUM

As the administrative capital of the European Community, Brussels is one of Europe's most international cities and has become a magnet for EC-watchers from Japan and elsewhere around the globe. In addition to the Japan Mission to the EC, a core group of Japanese government officials from the Embassy of Japan, the Japan External Trade Organization (JETRO) and other bodies can be found in the city which is also the country capital of Belgium.

Belgium's business associations with Japan go back a long time. Japan's trading companies had a presence there as early as the 1950s. Marubeni

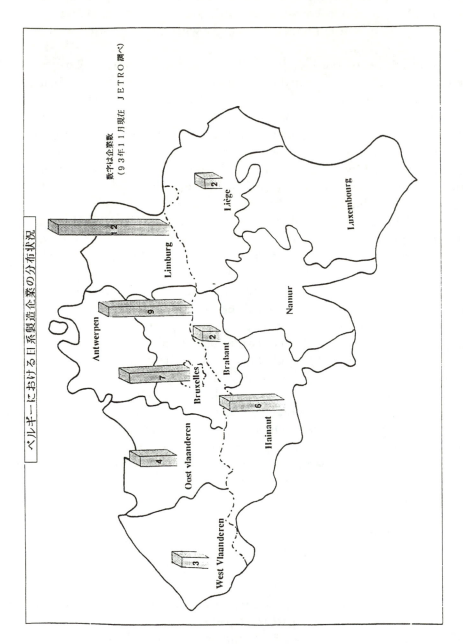

Map showing the location of Japanese manufacturers in Belgium.

Benelux SA, for example, began its activities in 1958 primarily with the import and export of textiles and machinery. Honda Belgium NV at Aalst, a subsidiary of Honda Motor Ltd in Japan, was in 1962 the first Japanese company to establish a Belgian base for the manufacture and sale of motorbikes. The majority of the 40 Japanese manufacturing companies in Belgium, however, arrived in the 1970s and 80s when the bubble economy was expanding rapidly. Today, those sectors most strongly represented are in the chemical, electronics and ceramics – stone and clay – industries.[47] In addition, there are some sixteen Japanese design centres and R&D bases.

By 1993 more than 250 Japanese firms had invested in Belgium, ranging from small liaison offices to large assembly and manufacturing operations and representing one of the highest percentages in Europe of wholly owned subsidiaries. Japanese market leaders with an investment of some kind in Belgium include such key names as Toyota, Nissan, Honda, Mazda, Komatsu, Pioneer, Panasonic, Hitachi and Sharp.

Japanese investment has been welcomed by the Belgian central government and Brussels region as well as by the regional governments of Flanders and Wallonia who are seeking to diversify local economies based on coal-mining, iron and steel and textiles.[48] The attraction of high technology-based industries and the employment opportunities generated by them has resulted in coordinated promotion drives aimed at Japan. Indeed, the Flanders government has set up a representative office in Osaka to this end.

Faced with the cultural diversity of Europe, Japanese firms and individuals in Belgium have yet further indigenous differences to contend with in the Flemish and French-speaking regions. On the whole, most Japanese manufacturing investment in Belgium is concentrated in Flemish areas, with good transport links and English language usage seen as prime attractions.[49] The Limburg region has been particularly successful in this regard.

A number of Japanese automotive companies have settled in and around Brussels along with representative offices of banks and securities houses, trading companies, airlines, news agencies, sales and service organizations. The proximity of Zaventem to Brussels Airport accounts for a further concentration there of Japanese transport and other firms. Incentive packages offered by special assistance areas such as Hainaut explains additional clusterings of Japanese companies elsewhere in Belgium.

There are currently 4,935 Japanese residents in Belgium, some 4,000 of which live in the Brussels area.[50] After London, Paris and Düsseldorf, Brussels can claim the largest concentration of Japanese in Europe. Unlike London and Paris, however, which have diverse Japanese populations including large numbers of students, Japanese residents in Brussels mainly consist of government workers, journalists and company employees and their families. Very few permanent expatriates are included in this number.

The Japanese live in a variety of Brussels suburbs including Auderghem, Watermael-Boitfort, Woluwe Saint-Pierre, Ixelles and Uccle. The location of the Brussels Japanese School at Auderghem has brought families with school-age children to this area. Outside of Brussels in the province of Limburg, Hasselt has become a further centre for the Japanese business community.

The Brussels Nihonjinkai or Japanese Club was established in 1966 with approximately 100 members.[51] As the Japanese presence in Belgium has increased, so too has its membership which has now reached 1,200. The Club acquired legal status in 1979 and took on the role of providing and administering educational facilities for the ever-growing number of expatriate Japanese children. A Japanese Saturday School had been in operation in Brussels since 1974. In 1979, however, Nihonjinkai acquired premises in Auderghem and founded the full-time Japanese School of Brussels with facilities for a maximum of 500 primary and junior high students.

In its networking capacity, Nihonjinkai stages and involves itself in a variety of events of a business, cultural and social nature throughout the year. Some of these are conducted in cooperation with the Belgium–Japan Association and Chamber of Commerce. Others, like the annual AGM party and visits to the Japanese school, are attempts to build bridges with the local Belgian community.

Despite its wider following, Nihonjinkai is first and foremost a Japanese club and, as such, contributes significantly to the support of the Japanese community. For its business membership, it issues a monthly newsletter and specialist reports and arranges topical seminars throughout the year. The school which it administers at Auderghem, meanwhile, acts as a focal point for all local Japanese.

The Parents and Teachers Association have produced a Japanese-language *Belgian Living Guide* for the use of the wider community. Listed within it are the ten Japanese restaurants in Brussels, the four Japanese supermarkets, two hotels, two bookshops, video library, two Japanese-speaking doctors, Japanese hairdressers and other services. Most of these are located in the vicinity of the Avenue Louise in the centre of Brussels and some are near to the Japanese School itself.

Not far from the latter is a Japanese bakery run by a Mr Ueno, husband of one of the Japanese-speaking Belgian women doctors in Brussels. Interesting cultural permutations can emerge from such personal tales.

A Japanese-language guide to living in Belgium.

Mr Ueno's shop, called Alli Gateaux, (a literal pun based on the Japanese expression for 'thank you', *arigato*) blends East and West in both form and content. A former employee of the renowned Belgian bakers, Wittamer, Mr Ueno caters, on the one hand, to Japanese tastes in bread and cakes, while exercising his locally learned skills for his Belgian clientele.

The preoccupations of the Japanese living in Belgium do not differ greatly from those concerns expressed in other parts of Europe. Education, healthcare, banking, shopping, travel, local pastimes and customs and language feature on most survival lists. In the case of Brussels, English and French are the languages that respectively come into play both at work and in society. While large companies, such as Toyota, tend to subsidise the costs of language lessons for employees and their families,in the main it is Japanese wives who take up such opportunities with their arguably greater need for French communication skills in daily life.

Japanese children attend either the Japanese School (which offers supplementary French tuition), international schools, or in some cases French-speaking state schools. French language education thus becomes, to a greater or a lesser degree, a normal part of their daily lives.

The Japanese find it relatively easy to operate within Belgian society and particularly within the international milieu of Brussels. English serves them well in business and, to varying degrees, in daily life. While their command of spoken English varies, it is nevertheless a language which can be understood and used in different parts of the country. A knowledge of English means access to English-language television as well as British and American newspapers, in addition to the Japanese alternatives. On

Brochure of the Japanese School of
Brussels.

the other hand, there is no English-language daily newspaper published
in Belgium, a fact which limits the Japanese grasp of local news and
current events.

While it is generally agreed that language limitations inhibit deeper
contact with the local community, many Japanese parents will not consider
French-speaking state schools as an option for their children, let alone
Flemish-speaking schools, because of their own inability to communicate
with teachers. Similarly, contact with business colleagues and neighbours
tends to remain on a superficial level due to language differences. The
forming of deeper friendships and links with the local community may well
depend on the improvement of language skills which, although adequate
for living and surviving in Belgium, do not allow for fuller integration
into society.

Various official organizations exist to aid in the process of integration.
The EC–Japan Club was founded in 1989 to provide members with opportunities for interaction and information exchange. Luncheons, conferences
and other social events as well as the publication of a monthly newsletter
help to expand existing business and social networks within the Brussels
community.

The Belgium Japan Association (BJA) and Chamber of Commerce has
also been effective in bringing the Belgians and the Japanese together.

Established in 1991, the BJA promotes both economic and cultural relations between Belgium and Japan through a wide range of activities, some organized in cooperation with Nihonjinkai. The Business and Cultural Committees of BJA regularly arrange conferences as well as social and cultural events and issue newsletters for the 300 members.

In November 1992, members of the BJA attended the opening of the Japanese garden in Hasselt followed by a tea party in the Flanders-Nippon Golf Club. Beyond Brussels, the Japanese community in the province of Limburg has similarly involved itself in such bilateral initiatives aimed at integration and cultural exchange. Limburg has an official link with Itami Prefecture in Japan and a Japan–Limburg Friendship Club was established several years ago. As a further commitment to the province, a Japanese school will be built there in the coming years.

Women's groups also play their part in creating links with the local community. Thé de l'Amitié (Tea of Friendship), a Belgian-led women's friendship circle, consists of some 100 Japanese and Belgian members who organize monthly social gatherings and events either at the Japanese Embassy or each other's homes. The planning of a paintings exhibition provides an annual focus of activity.

Another women's initiative, Petits-Pois, is a network for young mothers initiated by Mrs Asahara, wife of a Toyota employee, in 1992. Begun as a vehicle for combating the isolation of living abroad with young children, the Petits-Pois free monthly newsletter circulates advice and information on many aspects of Belgian life. While aimed at the Japanese wives' community, Petits-Pois functions with support from both Japanese and Belgian volunteers. Each issue of the newsletter contains practical tips on such diverse matters as choosing wine and using a fireplace, as well as information on local festivals and events, a practical tour guide, a nature column and news digest.

The lively nature of Petits-Pois and its newsletter reflect the changed circumstances of Japanese postings abroad. The senior company employees and their wives who were formerly sent overseas to establish new operations brought with them a burden of responsibility for purveying an 'appropriate' image of Japan abroad. Petits-Pois conjures up the spirit of these younger generation ambassadors from Japan who are less inhibited in their attempts to come to terms with foreign cultures.

Most Japanese adapt readily to life in Belgium. Brussels, as an international capital, is both cosmopolitan and convenient. Belgians are seen as easy-going and accepting of foreigners and the Japanese have had few problems with racial discrimination or with crime. The excellent cuisine is much enjoyed and the Japanese services infrastructure ensures that native alternatives are

ご自由にお持ち帰りください
❦❦❦ 無料 ❦❦❦

1994年 1月 1日 NO. 16

編集・発行：a.s.b.l.PETITS-POIS
CHAUSSEE DE NEERSTALLE 89,1190 BRUXELLE
連絡先 ： 電話：0二・七三一・五一九三（上西方） ファックス：0二・三七六・二八二一（神野方）

生活情報紙

明けましておめでとうございます

おかげさまでプチポワは２回目のお正月を迎えました。今年も楽しい紙面を作っていきたいと思っておりますので引き続きご支援のほど、お願い申し上げます。

さて、今年初めの話題は、食いしん坊なテーマがお得意のプチポワにふさわしく、おせち料理の由来を取り上げてみました。２ページ以下にこの文を英・仏・蘭語に訳してありますので是非こちらのお友達にも紹介してあげてください。

私たち日本人にとってお正月は、年間を通じて最も重要な行事です。

１月１日の朝には、家族一同が集まって、お屠蘇・お雑煮・おせち料理をいただきます。おせち料理は元旦から包丁などを使わないようにと、いろいろな種類のごちそうを大晦日までに重箱に詰めておきます。日本独特のものかと思っていましたが、ルーツは中国。その昔、中国では、お正月は神様がいらっしゃる日とされており、お供え物をして、五穀豊饒・家内安全を祈り、また当時を思えば大変滋養に富み、めったに口にすることのできないおいしい食べ物をいただいて鋭気を養い、健康を願う習慣がありました。これが日本に伝わって、そこに日本人の知恵、食への感覚が加味されて、今のような形へと受け継がれてきたのです。

おせち料理のひとつひとつには、小さな願いが込められています。

- ごまめ（カタクチイワシの幼魚を干したもの）＝マメに働いていけますように。
  また漢字で「五万米」と書いてお米の豊作を、別称「田作り」と言って田畑の豊作を願う、ご祝儀用の食べものです。
- ごぼう＝土の中に深く根付いていることから、家の基盤が揺るぐことのないように。
- 昆布巻＝「こんぶ」と「喜ぶ」の語呂合わせから。
- 栗（勝栗（かちぐり。鬼皮・波皮を除き、干したもの））勝ち戦にちなんで、武士が好んだ縁起物。
- れんこん＝穴が開いていることから、見通しが良くなりますように。
- 数の子＝子孫繁栄。
- 海老＝その形状から、腰が曲がるまで長寿をお祝いできますように。
- 黒豆＝マメに暮らせますように。
- 慈姑（くわい。水田栽培の多年草）早く芽が出ますように。

こちらの人達は、クリスマスイブの夜に家族つどってごちそうをしますね。その後ミサに出掛ける人もいます。私たちはお正月に帰省しますし、初詣もします。この時期は、世の東西を問わず、厳かに、そして楽しく暖かく過ごしたい頃なのかも知れませんね。

The *Petits-Pois* newsletter, produced by Japanese company wives in Brussels.

readily available for the homesick. The Belgian weather and Belgian drivers provide some cause for complaint but, minor criticisms aside, the Japanese enjoy their stay in Belgium and find it an ideal base from which to travel to many other parts of Europe.

The lifestyle of the Japanese community may seem a far cry from the world of Brussels bureaucrats and the official involvements that dominate Japan's relations with the European Community. When the EC–Japan Joint Declaration was signed in 1991, it was agreed that Japan and Europe should look beyond the economic preoccupations of trade issues and adopt a wider common agenda. The experience of the Japanese community in Belgium is at the very least making 'Europe' a more accessible entity and home away from home.

THE JAPANESE IN SPAIN

It was through Spain and Portugal that Japan first established relations with the West in the mid-sixteenth century. The missionaries and traders who ventured forth to Japan carved out their respective spheres of influence and, in turn, contributed select features of southern European culture to Japan. The distinction between southern versus northern Europe grew in the Japanese mind through trade with the Dutch and through the official missions and individual travels of the Japanese in Europe in the nineteenth century.

The journal of the Iwakura mission of 1871 spoke of 'an industrious, prosperous north and an indolent, impoverished south' of Europe and of the national differences that arose from differences in climate and terrain.[52] The southern countries were perceived as 'backward' with national development in Spain particularly hampered by the abuses of religious power.[53] Historical associations and the search for European models for industrial modernization relegated Spain to the minor league in the eyes of the Japanese.

Only in recent years have commercial interests between Spain and Japan become realigned through tourism and foreign investment. In 1993, a total of 250,000 Japanese tourists visited Spain.[54] The lure of a good climate and a rich cultural heritage have brought ever-increasing numbers of Japanese students and mature travellers to different parts of the country.

Japanese foreign direct investment in Spain dates back to the late 1960s and early 70s when trading companies and manufacturing operations were established in Madrid and Barcelona. Japan's interests in Spain were asserted with the steady procession of trading companies that came into the country, beginning with Marubeni in 1970, Mitsui in 1971 and Mitsubishi in 1973.

Manufacturing investment was slow to develop for political and infrastructural reasons but Spain's low-wage economy nevertheless proved attractive to some Japanese firms. Sanyo Electric Trading Co. set up a colour television manufacturing operation in Barcelona in 1969 and now attributes 20 per cent of its European sales to Spain.[55] Fujitsu's joint venture with Spain's PTT Telefonica to manufacture computers and printers at Malaga began in 1973, and Canon established a presence in Madrid in 1974.

Post-Franco Spain saw a proliferation of Japanese investments in the 1980s. Sony began colour television production at its factory in Catalonia in 1982, while joint ventures were entered into by Nissan and Motor Iberica in Barcelona in 1980, and by Suzuki and Land Rover at Linares in Andalusia in 1984. The high proportion of Japanese joint ventures in Spain have provided relatively safe means of entry into the Spanish market through association with long-standing partners.

Some 47 per cent of Japanese investment in Spain is concentrated in the capital, Madrid, with its numerous banks, insurance companies and finance houses.[56] The Bank of Tokyo opened its Madrid office in 1979 and was followed in the 1980s and 90s by many of Japan's leading financial institutions and services. Most manufacturers have settled in Barcelona and the surrounding region of Catalonia, Spain's industrial heartland, where 28 per cent of Japanese investment in the country has been made.[57] The regional government of Catalonia has actively promoted such investment and its success rate has been attributed to the reputation of the local Catalan workforce for high productivity and good labour relations. The Barcelona Olympics in 1992 expanded the region's communications network while the excellent port and airport facilities of Barcelona have strengthened Catalonia's image as a gateway to other markets in Europe, of increasing importance following Spain's admission to the European Community in 1986. Beyond Madrid and Barcelona, further Japanese investment has been made in the regions of Andalusia and Valencia and in the Canary Islands.

Regional differences in the quality of the Spanish workforce were highlighted in 1994 with the lengthy strike at Suzuki's Land Rover-Santana plant at Linares in Andalusia. The commonly held view of Andalusia as a dependency culture has been echoed by the Japanese who baldly state: 'In Andalusia, they simply do not work!' Certainly Spain's unwieldy employment legislation has created difficulties for Japanese firms seeking lay-offs in a period of recession. While many would identify the root cause of the Land Rover-Santana labour conflict as regionally based, for others it has drawn attention to the wider difficulties facing Japanese employers in Spain.

Japanese direct investment into Spain peaked in the run-up to Expo '92 in Seville and the 1992 Summer Olympics in Barcelona. Its subsequent decline has been attributed to the impact of the recession, the dramatic rise in Spanish wage rates and the fall in the value of the peseta.[58] Despite the recent downturn, with 64 Japanese manufacturers operating in the country as of January 1994, Spain can still claim the fourth largest concentration of Japanese manufacturing investment in Europe.[59] Meanwhile, the aggregation of manufacturing and non-manufacturing investment has brought more than 170 Japanese companies to Spain including 26 R&D centres.

Spain's Japanese community has grown in direct proportion to Japanese investment. In 1993, the population of 4,532 Japanese were divided between Madrid, Barcelona and other smaller centres of manufacturing and real estate investment. While predominantly a business community, Spain accommodates further numbers of Japanese government employees, journalists, students and artists. Of the 2,476 Japanese citizens registered with the Embassy of Japan in Madrid in 1993, nearly 46 per cent represented businessmen and their families, in comparison with the 1,821 Japanese registered with the Consulate in Barcelona, two-thirds of whom were from the business sector.[60]

The Japanese in Madrid live in the north-west zone in such areas as Vaguada, Mira Sierra and Mahada Honda where the presence of the full-time Japanese school exerts the usual appeal for families. Traffic congestion and distance have attracted company directors without children away from such Japanese suburbs to housing in the centre of Madrid.

Barcelona's Japanese community can be found to the north of the city in the areas of Pedralbes, Les Tres Torres and Bonanova. The Japanese School, located 10 kilometres to the north-east of Barcelona, and its bus route, again provide a logical inducement. As more than 90 per cent of children attend the school, the concentration of Japanese in these areas is particularly high.[61]

Facilities for the Japanese in Madrid and Barcelona are comparable. There are about twelve Japanese restaurants in Madrid and fifteen in Barcelona. Each city has a small selection of specialist food shops and the main Japanese department stores are represented. A branch of *Mitsukoshi* on a prominent corner of Madrid's Gran Via caters to tourists and residents alike while *Sogo* has recently opened its well-appointed showcase for Japanese goods and fashion close to Barcelona's port facilities. Sogo responded to the niche in the Japanese residents' market created when Mitsukoshi Ltd and Isetan Co. withdrew from Barcelona in the post-Olympics period.

There are additional business organizations that look after the interests of the Japanese companies and schools in Spain. Nihonjinkai was established

The *OCS News* bulletin is produced
for the Japanese community in Spain.

in Madrid in 1991 while branches of Suiyokai have been in operation in
Madrid and Barcelona for over twenty years. No bilateral clubs for the Japanese and the Spanish exist and, on the whole, interaction with the Spanish
community is on a relatively formal level. Academic and cultural interest in
Japan in Spain is similarly limited in comparison with other parts of Europe.

For the Japanese company employee and his family, Spain represents
a pleasurable posting, usually of four to five years duration, in lifestyle
terms. The climate is good and leisure facilities such as golf courses and,
in Barcelona, nearby beaches contribute to the quality of life. The Japanese
adapt well to the Spanish diet, rich in offerings of fresh fish, and to the
different eating rhythms of the Spanish.

For Japanese wives, Spain's cultural appeal is realized in language study,
cookery classes and lessons in flamenco dancing and local crafts. Barcelona's
Japanese women publish their own newsletter, *Barna Tsushin*, and operate
a Japanese lending library for books.

While many Japanese business families adhere closely to their company
groups, for others who have previously lived in South America, contact
with the Spanish community is more regular. The common practice of
sending Japanese with South American experience to Spain has created
a sub-culture within the Japanese community of those who can and do
communicate and adapt readily to Latin culture.

25. MAR. 1994
No. 7
Cabestany, 24, 4o, 2a.
08014 BARCELONA
FAX(93)439-0798
無料

ばるな通信　春の号
BARNA TSUSHIN

SEMANA SANTA
カーニバルから四旬節まで

LA QUARESMA Y DOMINGO DE RAMOS

四旬節・枝の主日(DOMINGO DE RAMOS)復活際前の日曜カーニバルのらんちき騒ぎの終わりと同時にイエスの砂漠での苦行から処刑、復活までの日々に由来する四旬節が始まります。

四旬節はカーニバルとは正反対にありとあらゆることを規制します。この四旬節の規制は非常に厳しいもので、旅行、観劇等に行くことはもちろん結婚、洗礼式等の公式の儀式さえも禁じられていました。そして、この期間の規則の反則者には、重い罰則が課せられました。

カーニバルをずんぐりむっくりとした愉快な修道僧とすれば、四旬節は鷲鼻で歯が抜けてすぼんだ唇の年寄りの半身魔女、半身修道女にたとえられます。

四旬節は七本の足として数えます。地方によっては、大きな乾燥鱈に七四の鰊を足の様に吊し、家の中、バルコニー、もしくは窓際にそれらの人形をぶら下げます。毎週日曜日には、一家の家長が一週間が過ぎた証に足を一本ずつ切り取って行くのです。

PASCUAという名は、ヘブライ語の過ぎ越し(PASHA(TRANSITO))を語源に持つと云われ、農耕作物の伐採と取り入れのための移動を意味します。

PASCUAは、LA PASCUA DE FLORIDA=開花、LA PASCUA DE GRANDA=実りの三日間のサイクルに分けられます。

葉緑 LA PASCUA DE FLORIDA=開花枝の主日(DOMINGO DE RAMOS=実りの三日)

セマナ・サンタの始まりは、清めの儀式から始まります。小さな村では、教会の司祭が小坊主の列を従え、塩と水で盛った印を家から家へと置いてまわります。その後、農家の人々と耕作物を神の加護があると祝福して行きます。これはイスラエル人がエジプトから逃げる前に生贄の小羊の血を家々の入り口に、印つけた事に由来するといわれます。教会の司祭の祝福に対して、民家の主婦達は、司祭や小坊主に食べ物と卵を与えました。(現在、お伏せとしては、現金が代表的になっています。)その見返りとして、悪霊から守ってくれるという訳です。

教会のミサの後、人々は外に出て歩きながら、PALMASで道を奇麗にしながら、歩いて行きます。月桂冠とオリーブの葉は昔から聖なる植物として、いろいろなシンボルに使われますが、もともとは、祈りの主婦達は

「開門、開門、中に入れてくれ、教会の扉を壊してしまうぞ」と歌います。でないと、教会の扉を壊してしまうぞ。

子供達はPALMASの先で地面を叩き、大人は月桂冠とオリーブの枝を手に教会に集まります。この日は、子供達は棕櫚を編んで作ったPALMASを、大人は棕櫚の葉と月桂冠とオリーブの葉で作った日曜日の枝の主日(DOMINGO DE RAMOS)は、民衆の間で広まったキリスト教信仰のなごりでもあります。

SEMANA SANTA それぞれの地方の伝統的な儀式と習慣を通して、時間を越えて続いてきた、特別な週間です。イエスの受難と処刑による死を、昨日のことであるかのように思い起こさせるものです。

最後に残った足を切り取ると、いよいよ復活際当日です。人形は吊されていた場所から外され、葬られるか、道で燃やされます。その後、PALMASは、イエスのエルサレムの町への入場を、人々が棕櫚の葉と月桂冠の枝を振って祝福した事とオリーブの葉を持って迎えています。同時に、復活際の聖週間の始まりでもあります。棕櫚、月桂樹、オリーブに象徴される枝(RAMO)は、実りと豊沃の象徴であり、ヨーロッパに共通の植物の成育の儀式を起源に持つと云われます。歴史家によると、オリーブの枝を語源に持つと

PASCUAという名は、ヘブライ語の過ぎ越しと

祷師によって使われ、雷を避ける力を持ち、永遠の命を意味しました。日曜日の枝の主日(DOMINGO DE RAMOS)は、悪霊の侵入から守るために翌年のカーニバルまで窓やバルコニーに置かれます。

一般に人々は祭りの前日にFERIASの市場を訪れます。人々は祭りの前にいろいろな場所でMERCADO DE RAMOS(RAMOS DE PALMASを買います)の様が見られます。RAMOSを始め、蝋燭、蜜ろう、ROSCAと云うドーナツの様なお菓子、パイナップル、ワイン等祭りの期間に必要なものを買い集めます。

(次頁に続く)

Barna Tsushin, the newsletter of Barcelona's Japanese women's community.

The Japanese acknowledge that Spanish is easier for them to pronounce than most other European languages. Lack of prior knowledge, however, does isolate many Japanese in Spain and can create problems in the workplace and in domestic life. English, while more commonly understood in Catalonia, is not widely spoken and Japanese speakers among the Spanish are certainly rare.

It has been argued that Latin peoples have an innate appreciation of the importance which the Japanese attach to the human relations context of business. While communication in English may result in a certain bluntness and directness of expression, the linguistic challenge presented by communication between the Japanese and the Spanish can allow both sides to admit to a breakdown in understanding without the same levels of embarrassment or pretence at having successfully conveyed meaning.[62]

While the Spanish lifestyle may provide a temporary respite from the Japanese pace of life, the more relaxed 'manana mentality' of the Spanish people gives rise to some frustration in business. Being late for appointments is an endemic tendency and 'workaholism' is an alien concept. As one Japanese said of the Spanish, 'They are very punctual, especially at the end of the working day'.

Family life always takes precedence over working life in Spain. The Japanese view of this cultural difference was expressed by a businessman in Madrid: 'The Spanish have a special talent for using their private hours . . . if Sunday and Tuesday are festival days, then most would not think twice about taking the Monday off work as well'.

In the workplace and beyond, the Spanish style has its critics amongst the Japanese. Some would decry the inefficiencies of the postal service and the banking system which the Spanish simply shrug and accept, and the Japanese find hard to tolerate. An underlying lack of a sense of urgency is perhaps the prime cause of Japanese frustrations in Spain.

A distinction is drawn by the Japanese between Spain as a place to work and as a place to live. From the latter perspective, it is one of the most preferred postings in Europe for businessmen and their families. The climate, food and warm hospitality of the Spanish people are rated high among its positive features. On the negative side, crime and the poor hygiene standards and graffiti in Spanish cities are commented upon by some but, by and large, do not greatly affect the Japanese living in their select suburbs. What they bring back to Japan after a five-year posting are essentially memories of a touristic experience tinged with insights into the southern European mentality.

A sense of nostalgia for Spain among the Japanese may derive from the historic ties that exist between the two nations. While the Spanish image

Madrid's *Suiyokai* Bulletin announcing the 1993 launch of 'Plan Japon'.

of Japan is largely centred on the high-tech goods of modern consumer culture, for the Japanese Spain is an exotic *mélange* of antiquated squares, palaces and lively and colourful flamenco dancers.

The Parque Espana which opened in Mie Prefecture in 1994 is yet another European-inspired Japanese theme park which has juxtaposed replicas of a two-thirds size Plaza Major, a *La Rambla*-inspired 'Spain Avenue' and many other simulations of Spanish places and things.[63] Parque Espana has thus recreated the tourist image which clings to Spain in Japan. The continuing popularity of such replica environments may suggest that Japanese interest in European culture is growing or that Japanese entrepreneurs are simply responding to an indigenous demand for an accessible and sanitized experience of Europe. For the Japanese who have lived in Spain, Parque Espana's historic settings, spotlessness and efficiency will leave some aspects of Spanish life unexplored.

Spain's entry into the European Community in 1986 has raised incomes and living standards and improved the country's infrastructure. Economic growth has been underpinned by the expansion of trade and of foreign investment from Japan. In 1993, the Spanish government launched '*Plan Japon*' to promote exchanges with Japan in the areas of technology transfer, trade, direct investment and tourism. If Spain has been late in resuming her early ties with Japan, in recent years she has taken a lead from other European nations who have identified Japan as a lucrative market and a desirable commercial and industrial partner.

5   The Japanization of Europe: Raw Fish, Wrestling and 'Just–in–Time'

The concept of 'Japanization' first emerged in Europe in the 1980s as Japanese industrial and management practices left their mark on the economies of a succession of countries playing host to foreign direct investment from Japan. For the Japanese, on the other hand, being in Europe was and remains an aspect of 'internationalization', another buzzword cum rallying-cry which expresses both Japan's global interests and the perceived need for her citizenry to adopt a wider view.

The notion of Japanese working methods as a kind of Holy Grail for industrial success lay behind the Japanization debate. Set against a tradition of Japan emulating the West, the 1970s and 80s witnessed an explosion of rhetoric on the secrets of Japan's remarkable economic achievement. Entrepreneurs like Toyoda Eiji, the Chairman of Toyota, and Morita Akio, 'Mr Sony', penned their autobiographies, while authors of various persuasions fixed upon the systems and the ethos which propelled the Japanese ever forward. The Japan-bashers were not far behind, but this too was an acknowledgement of Japan's global status as the lessons so avidly learned from the West in the Meiji period and the postwar years came to be transmogrified into a model for the West to follow.

In Oliver and Wilkinson's UK-based study, *The Japanization of British Industry*, the parameters of Japanization are succinctly defined:

> We used the expression 'Japanization' as an umbrella term to refer to the process by which some aspects of UK industry appeared to be converging towards a Japanese-style model of management practice. This process encompassed two strands – the emulation of Japanese manufacturing methods by Western manufacturers and also the increasing volume of Japanese direct manufacturing investment in Western economies.[1]

The Sun celebrates the Japanization of Britain, 23 October 1991 (MCH).

The manufacturing and organizational methods which have become the subject of close analysis in Europe and America include the operation of quality circles, total quality management, 'just-in-time' production systems and a range of Japanese employment practices.[2] Examples of Japanization can be found across Europe, but Britain has been particularly influenced by the scale of Japanese manufacturing investment in her midst. In his book, *Japanese Manufacturing Investment in Wales*, Max Munday illustrates the use of the Japanese model by British industry:

> Jaguar Cars and Thorn EMI have both learnt extensively from Japan in many areas of factory organization. Wedgewood Potteries now use 'Japanese' methods for production and quality control. Both Ford and Xerox/Rank Xerox have also undergone organizational change relating to the emulation of Japanese company working methods.[3]

For many firms, the experience of Japanization has yielded positive results, yet transplanting Japanese industrial methods onto foreign soil has not been without its problems. Banners proclaiming 'We're Brits, not Nips' were brandished by striking Ford workers in 1988, opposed to the company's adoption of Japanese-style flexible work practices. Ford UK first launched its 'After Japan' programme following a trip to Japan by Ford Europe's President, Bill Hayden. The view of 'the Japanese challenge as being based on cheap labour and a sheltered domestic market' was supplanted by:

recognition that the Japanese management style was diamet-
rically opposed to the western model, the key being management by consent rather than control, and the mobilisation
of worker knowledge behind company goals rather than the
elimination of all vestiges of employee discretion.[4]

The introduction of quality circles was seen by Ford as the first step on the
road to Japanization, but manufacturing unions resisted this latest Japanese
export as a threat to the more traditional bargaining mechanisms of British
industrial life.

Rover's long-standing relationship with the Japanese carmaker, Honda,
brought about further collaboration between British and Japanese industry
on the development and production of new car ranges which resulted in
the adoption of Japanese production methods and management practices.
Under the terms of a 'New Deal' agreement reached between the
company and its employees in 1992, Rover introduced such 'Japanese'
features as continuous improvement, total flexibility, training initiatives,
quality action teams and increased employee responsibility.

Across the automobile industry, the need to compete against the
Japanese to survive has been a spur to Japanization. As one Rover
spokesman stated:

> We must have a level playing field in terms of processes and
> working practices if we are to succeed against our competitors,
> particularly the Japanese.[5]

Jaguar Cars began its 'Pursuit of Perfection' campaign in 1980 by
analysing the strengths of its main competitors – among them, the Japanese.
Japanese-style practices, including quality circles, were employed in the
implementation of the programme's main objectives:

> to improve in-company communications and involve em-
> ployees at all levels of problem-solving, to improve product
> quality and reliablity in a measurable way, in comparison with
> the competition, and to reduce operating costs in all areas,
> particularly production.[6]

Jaguar's success in quality improvement drew attention to those Japanese
work practices and attitudes that might effectively be transferred to a
British setting.

The debate still rages as to what can and cannot be adapted from the
wider culture of business in Japan to the specific circumstances of a
manufacturing firm in the West. Time and experience have eroded the
simple black-and-white distinctions between industrial models and the
lessons seemingly implicit in their success. Quality control circles have
become synonymous with good Japanese management practice but owe

their origins to such American management gurus as W.E. Deming and J.M. Juran whose ideas never quite caught on in Europe until they were reinvented by the Japanese. There is too the issue of the higher status accorded to manufacturing industry in Japan as compared with many parts of Europe, against which the detail of such areas of emulation must be set.

Britain's premier role in attracting Japanese manufacturing investment and her pursuit of technology exchange with Japan has placed her firmly at the centre of the Japanization debate. In other parts of Europe, however, as with Mitsubishi Motors and Volvo's tie-up in the Netherlands, partnerships with the Japanese are spreading the sphere of Japan's impact upon western industry. Japanese production bases in Europe have further focused attention upon differentials in quality and productivity standards and heightened the need for French, German and other manufacturers to learn from the Japanese or, at the very least, to adopt a 'best of both worlds' approach to the management of change.

The emotive response to Japan's incursions into the European motor industry has been attributed to a number of factors, both concrete and symbolic. The restrictive Japanese car import quotas imposed in France and Italy reflect the protectionist policies of these governments, but there is a deeper meaning too to be gleaned from such onslaughts. In the view of one author,

> The home-produced automobile is an institution, a tradition,
> a symbol of industrial strength; and needless to say, a source
> of considerable employment, both direct and indirect. It also
> plays a key role in European social developments, particularly
> in industrial relations.[7]

As markets have been won and lost, the high visibility of Japanese cars on European roads – like the electronic goods that dominate the households and high-street shops of the West – bring a consciousness of Japan's seemingly unbeatable industrial prowess into the realm of everyday life.

The ubiquity of the Japanese presence ranges from such potent yet everyday objects as motor cars and video recorders to the Japanese ownership of enterprises and institutions which seem redolent of European culture and tradition. The purchases of the Courrèges fashion house in France and Turnberry Golf Club in the UK are but two examples of this phenomenon which have occurred in recent years. Beyond the impact of Japanese manufacturing industry, Japanization can be interpreted in the broader context of Japan's conspicuous consumption abroad in the prosperous 1980s and of the growing influence within Europe of Japanese culture, taste and style.

   A wealth of Japanese festivals, exhibitions and events has taken place in
various parts of Europe in the last decade or so and familiarity with the
full spread of Japanese culture, from *kabuki* to *karaoke*, has grown in direct
proportion to investment from Japan. Where once Japan and China were
indistinguishable entities in the European mind, a clearly defined identity
for Japan has been forged in recent years. The 'Japan Style' exhibition at
London's Victoria and Albert Museum in 1980 brought the popular culture
and craft tradition of Japan into the public arena just as the provocatively
titled traditional craftwork display, 'How to Wrap Five Eggs', or its Italian
variant, *'Come Impacchettare Cinque Uova'*, made its way across Europe
from 1981. In this climate, exhibitions of *manga*, contemporary Japanese
comics, were soon competing for attention with the high art products of
a bygone age.

   Japan's reopening to trade with the West in the 1850s resulted in her
art and industrial products being put on show in a host of international
exhibitions from Philadelphia to Vienna in the latter decades of the
nineteenth century. Trade, investment and the flourishing academic and
cultural links between Britain and Europe have repeated and intensified
this process over a century later.

   Britain's 'Great Japan Exhibition' (Art of the Edo Period 1600–1868),
held at the Royal Academy of Arts in London between 1981 and 1982,
marked a kind of turning-point in Japan's profile in Europe. As the
foreword of the exhibition catalogue explained:

> Since 1945 Japan has tended to look primarily towards the
> United States of America and it is here that the closest political,
> economic and cultural ties have developed. However, the
> 1970s have seen greatly increased political, trading and, most
> recently, investment links between Japan and Europe . . . that
> mutual suspicions do remain is partly due to an ignorance of
> historical and cultural developments, and it is in this context
> that the Great Japan Exhibition at the Royal Academy is
> taking place.[8]

The focus upon the Edo period provided an historical framework within
which to view Japanese society and culture at a time when Japan was once
again expanding her intercourse with the outside world.

   The close collaboration between the Japanese and British governments,
industry and the art establishment in planning and executing the exhibition
and its highly successful reception by both press and public alike paved the
way for future cultural exchange between Japan and Europe. Meanwhile,
its design by the eminent architect, Kurokawa Kisho, created another level
of interplay between the art worlds of East and West.

Programme for Europalia '89, 'Japan
in Belgium'.

When the Great Japan Exhibition was opened in London in 1981,
Britain had a small but growing number of Japanese production bases
and a Japanese population (mainly centred in the capital) of some 13,000
residents (as compared with 54,000 in 1993). There were clusters of
Japanese restaurants in the centre of London predictably contiguous to the
Embassy of Japan and to the offices of Japan Air Lines, the Japan External
Trade Organization (JETRO) and the major Japanese firms. Catering to an
élite business community, such 'temples' to Japanese cuisine were beyond
the budgetary reach of the ordinary citizen and reflected the exclusive
image of the Japanese themselves as aloof and distant aliens in a foreign
land. This image did not change overnight but, with the Great Japan
Exhibition, the grandest and costliest exhibition ever staged at the Royal
Academy, came an acknowledgement of Japan's global importance and
of the growing cultural as well as economic relationship with Britain and
Europe.

Throughout the 1980s, the Japan Foundation and other Japanese and
European bodies sponsored a succession of exhibitions and theatrical
events. The variety of the offerings reflected the burgeoning curiosity
about Japan in Europe which did not confine itself to the traditional arts
but to the full gamut of popular and avant-garde taste. Tours of *kabuki*
and *bunraku* continued to command a following but were juxtaposed with

performances of *koto* drumming and the more experimental *buto* dance. Meanwhile, the work of the Japanese director Ninagawa Yukio brought contemporary Japanese theatre to the European stage.

Japonisme, the nineteenth-century cult of Japan in Europe, once gave rise to a similar surge of interest in Japan. The same cities which today play host to large Japanese business communities still bear the remnants of this earlier fascination with Japan. The Tour Japonaise built at Laeken in Brussels a hundred years ago now serves as a museum which regularly exhibits aspects of Japanese culture to local Belgian and Japanese visitors. Likewise in The Hague, the Japanese garden at Clingendael speaks of the admiration felt by Maguèrite, Baroness van Brienen, for the culture of Japan. Britain, too, has its historical 'monuments' to Japanese taste. Wealthy Victorian and Edwardian visitors to Japan returned home with an enthusiasm for Japanese architecture and gardening which were soon being imitated on British soil. The Japanese Tea House at Heale House Gardens in Wiltshire, brought from Japan in the 1880s, still stands today and there is a further variety of Japanese gardens which have survived from the turn-of-the-century period including those at Cottered in Hertfordshire, at Newstead Abbey near Nottingham and at Tatton Park in Cheshire.

Attention has been drawn to these reflections from the past through more recent encounters between Japan and Europe. In Paris, a major exhibition on the theme of '*Japonisme*' was organized at the Grand Palais in 1988. There have been similar exhibitions at Leiden in the Netherlands and in Vienna where '*Verborgene Impressionen, Japonismus in Vienna*' was held in 1990 and in London where 'Japan and Britain: An Aesthetic Dialogue 1850–1930' took place at the Barbican Art Gallery between 1991 and 1992. In the autumn of 1993, the Martin Gropius Building in Berlin was the setting for yet another impressive inter-cultural visual arts display, 'Japan and Europe 1543–1929'.

Ever-closer economic relations with Japan have been the backdrop to an intensification and diversification of cultural activity as, in addition to art exhibitions and theatrical performances, Japanese musical, dance, cinematic and sporting events have come to Europe on an increasingly frequent basis. As Japanese investment peaked in the late 1980s, a spate of major arts festivals brought Japanese cultural exposure in Europe to a parallel crescendo.

The year 1989 saw Belgium's prestige annual arts festival, the *Europalia*, focused on Japan, the first time that a non-Western country had ever inspired its theme. The *Europalia*'s 'Japan in Belgium' festival took place from September to December 1989 and, in this three-month period, brought the ancient and modern culture of Japan, in its many forms, to

Festival Culturel du Japon in Paris 1993.

Brussels and beyond. Highlights of the festival included exhibitions of Japanese Buddhist art, *Namban* art, and art and technology in Japan. The theatrical spread was equally wide with traditional displays of *no* and *kabuki* balanced by the work of the Ninagawa Company and performances of *buto*. Laser art, the martial arts, Japanese tea ceremony and a kimono fashion show contributed to the spectacle whereby Japan emphatically made its presence felt in Belgium.

Japan again took centre stage in Europe as the theme country for Germany's Frankfurt Book Fair held in the autumn of 1990. A coordinated programme of events brought a cross-section of Japanese exhibitions and performances into the literary frame.

In Britain, the 100th anniversary of the Japan Society in 1991 offered the impetus for a celebration of the arts and culture of Japan that was organized on an unprecedented scale. The 'Japan Festival 1991' was launched, exactly ten years after the Great Japan Exhibition, with over 350 events taking place over the autumn and winter of 1991–2 at more than 200 venues throughout the UK. At a cost of more than £20 million. and funded by both Japanese and British sponsors, 'the greatest celebration of another country's culture ever held in Britain' took place. In the previous year, 'UK 90', a major British festival, had brought the arts of Britain to Japan, aiming to demonstrate their full regional breadth and vitality to the Japanese. The Japan Festival 1991 similarly adopted as its guiding principles the dismantling of stereotypes and the having of 'fun', flagging up the high art as well as the 'raw fish and wrestling' faces of Japan. According to its chairman, Sir Peter Parker, it strove 'to make Japan more accessible, more understandable and more enjoyable to the British people'.[9] Advance publicity exhorted the public to 'Prepare to Be Astonished' and this they were as a 'Grand Sumo Tournament' was staged at London's Royal Albert Hall, an interactive 'Robotics Japan' exhibition drew crowds at the Science Museum and Japanese 'samurai' archers galloped on horseback through Hyde Park in a re-creation of the medieval spectacle of *Yabusame*. 'Visions of Japan', the highly innovative centrepiece exhibition which attracted a quarter of a million visitors to the Victoria and Albert Museum brought Japan into sharp cultural focus, juxtaposing past, present and future visions by three leading Japanese architects within a framework set by Isozaki Arata of the continuity and contrasts of Japanese life.

Outside London, in the North of England, Northern Ireland, Scotland and Wales the Japan Festival reached out to communities that, through Japanese investment, had become used to another kind of Japanese presence in their midst. Japanese *sumo* wrestlers set their weighty talents against the more diminutive skills of traditional Cumbrian wrestlers, Japanese businessmen resident in the provinces experienced Japan's *No* theatre for the first time and on a British stage, and schoolchildren throughout the land learned about Japan from Japanese company wives participating in the festival's education scheme. The festival left its mark upon many people who saw Japan in all its different dimensions, including the UK's Japanese residents who had the opportunity to scrutinize their own country's image from the perspective of the British.

Another prestige vehicle for Japanese culture in Europe was furnished by 'Expo '92', the Seville Universal Exposition held in Spain in 1992. The impressive wooden *Pabellon de Japon* (Japan Pavilion) at the centre of the exposition site was designed by the renowned Japanese architect, Ando Tadao, and organized by the Japan External Trade Organization (JETRO). Visitors to the Japan Pavilion were impressed by both its stark sweeping lines and its scale. It was one of the largest wooden buildings to have been constructed in the last fifty years and its structural supports were held in place without nails, a traditional feature of Japanese building design.

The theme of the Pavilion was 'The Discovery of the Origin and the Future of Japan', providing the opportunity to explore past and present, tradition and modernity, in its inner spaces. The image of the Japanese as a nation of borrowers was openly challenged in its stated aim:

> to make the visitor understand that this amalgam of ideas and facts (as represented in the contents of the Pavilion) is not due to any process if reproduction or imitation, but rather to the fruit born out of Japanese history itself.[10]

Inside the pavilion, the history of Japan's early links with Spain and Portugal were featured, as was the evolution of Japanese cultural forms.

The *pièce de résistance*, a revolving theatre, offered a vantage point from which to view a high-tech blend of Japan's past, present and future in the animated company of Sasuke, a legendary Japanese Ninja, and Don Quixote and Sancho Panza. In Expo'92 Japan set out to impress and to inform and, in so doing, put some stereotypes to rest, but not all. The Summer Olympic Games in Barcelona in 1992 witnessed another cultural export from Japan to Spain in the Sant Jordi Sports Palace, designed by the architect, Isozaki Arita.

Throughout Europe the platforms for Japanese cultural contact multiplied with the expansion of support from official and unofficial organizations and corporate sponsors in the late 1980s and early 90s. 'Japan Weeks', coordinated by the Embassy of Japan and Japan Foundation, designed to introduce Japanese culture and society to the general public, brought artistic and educational highlights to a host of major European cities. A full programme of events was staged in different parts of the Netherlands in the autumn of 1991. A Düsseldorf 'Japan Week' took place in the summer of 1992. In Marseille, a 'Japan Week' extravaganza brought together 2,800 Japanese performers in a major showcase for Japanese culture.

The Embassy of Japan and UNESCO joined forces in the spring of 1993 to present the '*Festival Culturel du Japon*' in Paris. Five weeks of exhibitions, films and performances reflected the ongoing popularity of Japanese art and culture in France, the home of *japonisme* and the European artistic discovery of Japan.

In June 1993, Japan returned to Belgium where the ten-day '*EC-Japan Fest*' was staged in Antwerp as part of a variety of cultural highlights marking the city's designation as European Cultural Capital for 1993. Kaifu Toshiki, Prime Minister of Japan at the time of the signing of the 1991 EC–Japan Joint Declaration, was Honorary Chairman of the *EC–Japan Fest* Committee and attached a particular significance to the cultural agenda. Kaifu pointed to a realization of the Declaration's aims:

> of broadening and spurring a qualitative leap forward in Japan-
> ese–European relations, which had been relatively distant and
> tending to tilt towards economic relations.[11]

Here, as in other parts of Europe, economic and cultural relations were seen to go hand in hand.

The acceleration of interest in Japanese culture in Europe proceeds apace. It may be that, from an official perspective, culture provides a safe sphere through which to channel more politically sensitive issues. The diplomacy of culture notwithstanding, the profile of Japan in Europe has in recent years been raised.

As the country in Europe with the largest share of Japanese investment

EC–Japan Fest, Antwerp '93. A week-long Japanese cultural festival held in Antwerp from 10–19 June 1993.

Belgian newspaper coverage of the EC–Japan Fest.

Go and *Ikebana*: Manifestations of Japanese cultural interests in the Netherlands.

and the most sizeable resident Japanese population, Britain demonstrates this characteristic to a greater degree. As one cultural ambassador from Japan recently observed:

> Interest in Japan among British people has increased amazingly in recent years. I have had a landlord who is interested in *haiku* and a plumber who is fond of *bonsai*; the owner of the Scottish hotel my family once dropped into had lived in Japan and, to my embarrassment, knew more than I did about some regions; my children's private English tutor is learning Japanese and . . . *sumo*, *karaoke* and Japanese food now seem part of daily conversation among British people.[12]

It is certainly true that Japanese 'culture', once the preserve of a narrow band of academic specialists and martial-arts and flower-arranging enthusiasts, has now been opened out to the wider community. There are restaurants offering Japanese food at palatable prices in various parts of the UK. The yuppie discovery of *sushi* has seen the popular rise of this raw fish delicacy in fast-food chains while the equivalent renaissance of the Japanese noodle has made the London establishment, Wagamama, an overnight success.

The economy and simplicity of Japanese design has brought *futon* (Japanese mattresses) to the high street while the 'no-brand goods' Muji shops now cater to all manner of austere taste. For those with brasher leanings, the *karaoke* phenomenon has made a considerable impact upon British life as the entertainment potential of the exported Japanese *karaoke* machine has blended seamlessly with the sing-along tradition of the British pub.

Clive James's sending up of Japanese games shows like 'Endurance' may have contributed a further stereotype of the Japanese to the existing panoply of distorted images but television has also introduced *sumo* wrestling into the British ken. Its considerable popularity has been attributed to factors of ritual, sport and sex appeal but, like *karaoke* and *sushi*, *sumo* is ceasing to be viewed as an alien import and is gradually becoming absorbed into the mainstream of British popular life.

Interest in Japanese cinema can be seen as a precursor of such present-day influences. Its popularity in the 1950s and 60s, particularly in Britain and France, brought a Japan of sensibilities rather than technological muscle into the realm of mass consumption. Kurosawa Akira's *Rashomon* won the San Marco/ Golden Lion Award at the 1951 Venice International Film Festival and later films by Mizoguchi Kenji and Ozu Yasujiro received further prestigious western awards. Art house cinema audiences embraced the stark black-and-white imagery and visually intriguing compositions that distinguished these Japanese imports as landmarks of avant-garde style. Their influence on a generation of European and American film-makers has been well-established. By the late 1980s, Kurosawa's *Ran* was being screened in cinemas everywhere to international accolades.

In the aftermath of the Japan Festival 1991, Japanese cultural initiatives in the UK have come to reflect a deeper public awareness of the diversity of Japanese art and entertainment. Hence 1994 brought Ninagawa Yukio to Britain to direct an English cast in a production of *Peer Gynt* while, on the stage of the London Coliseum, the all-singing, all-dancing, all-female Japanese review company, *Takarazuka*, demonstrated that the culture of Radio City Music Hall and the Rockettes also has its place in Japan. The prurient interest shown by the British press in the cross-dressing and ambiguous sexuality of the *Takarazuka* troupe provided yet another dimension in the rebounding of stereotypes between East and West.

Japan's close ties with Britain have given rise to numerous events and displays, but the last ten years have also witnessed the emergence of a more permanent legacy in the sponsorship of major cultural installations by the Japanese. The Victoria and Albert Museum's Toshiba Gallery of Art opened in 1986 and the British Museum's Japanese Galleries followed in 1990 as the result of over £4 million in Japanese sponsorship. The Kyoto Garden in London's Holland Park was the Kyoto Chamber of Commerce and Industry's contribution to the Japan Festival 1991 and, as such, was officially opened by the festival's joint Patrons, HRH the Prince of Wales and HIH the Crown Prince of Japan in the autumn of 1991. Using local materials, Japanese gardeners and British contractors worked together to realize the Japanese design. As on the factory floor, this collaborative exercise achieved successful results and, in the process, brought the Japanese and the British into direct and meaningful contact.

Further legacies of the Japan Festival lay in the creation of the Japan Festival Fund, providing annual awards for outstanding achievement in enhancing the British understanding of Japanese culture, the Japan Festival Education Trust for the continuation of the educational activities so innovatively launched in 1991 and the Japan Society Awards for contributions in the field of Anglo-Japanese relations. Japanese sponsorship, both public and private, has helped to fuel such initiatives and to foster the Japanese arts and culture in Britain. In this respect, the London-based Great Britain Sasakawa Foundation and the Daiwa Anglo-Japanese Foundation, through their scholarships and grants, play an ongoing supportive role.

At the opening of the Daiwa Foundation Japan House in London in July 1994, the Foreign Secretary, Douglas Hurd, quoted from the UK-Japan 2000 Group's recent report on UK–Japan relations which stated that despite the 'explosive growth of interest by Britons in things Japanese . . . and the continuing strong interest in Britain from many Japanese . . . a critical mass of self-sustaining growth in mutual awareness and understanding has (not) yet been achieved'.[13]

The Daiwa Foundation's establishment of a permanent base in London for Japanese cultural, educational, academic and other professional exchanges has its parallels in other parts of Europe where Japan House-type developments have taken place with Japanese government support. There are similar centres in Berlin, Cologne and Rome, and, in Paris, the *Maison de la Culture du Japon*, designed by the British architect Kenneth Armstrong, will be opened in 1996.

The study of Japan in Europe has flourished with the expansion of investment and business links. Between 1984 and 1990, for example, the number of French people learning Japanese increased from 2,600 to 7,740[14] while the British total has recently been estimated at 14,000.[15] These figures apply to the full breadth of Japanese courses offered by schools, adult education institutes and higher education establishments. In Germany, the number of students enrolled in Japanese Studies programmes has multiplied by more than ten times over the last ten years.[16] Academic centres for Japanese Studies can be found throughout Europe with older universities like Leiden offering Japanese Studies programmes which hark back to long-standing historic ties.

In Britain, Sir Peter Parker's 1987 report, *Speaking for the Future*, recommended an increase in government funding for Japanese studies. Its successful implementation resulted in the spreading outwards of Japanese studies from the original four centres at Cambridge, Oxford, Sheffield and the London School of Oriental and African Studies and a mushrooming of courses in Japanese. Between 1987 and 1993, the number of university students taking some form of Japanese language course virtually quadrupled to 1914 and there are now 42 universities offering single or joint honours degrees featuring the study of Japan or Japanese.[16]

The development of the field has also seen the founding of the British Association for Japanese Studies in 1974 and the European Association for Japanese Studies (EAJS) in 1973. Japanese Studies Associations are in operation in seven European countries and more than 850 Japan specialists are currently estimated to be working throughout Europe.[17]

Japan's imprint upon Europe encompasses economic, social and cultural ties. Twinning arrangements exist between Tokyo and Paris. In the UK, as of 1993, six Japanese city twinning arrangements were in place. The first of these to be established, between Gillingham in Kent and Yokosuka (Kanagawa) and Ito (Shizuoka), commemorated William Adams's

Karaoke choirs — a new English way of life?

Pub-goers are singing along to the tune of ringing tills

By KATHARINE CRACKNELL
SPECIAL TO THE JOURNAL

LONDON — Condemned by some as noise pollution, an addiction by others, *karaoke* is catching on in the UK.

Karaoke, which means "empty orchestra" in Japanese, comprises recorded pop tunes minus the vocals and the equipment allowing consumers to sing along.

Long popular in Japan, karaoke, or "kariokь," as it is pronounced here, "is becoming more popular than we could ever have hoped," says John Bamford, spokesman for Pioneer High Fidelity GB, a subsidiary of Japan's Pioneer Electronic Corp, the top karaoke equipment maker. However, a spokesman for Singing Machine Co., Pioneer's main karaoke equipment distributors in this country, says, "Singing is an English way of life, too."

The Japanese karaoke lover, however, might not recognize the English version. It is not individuals singing solo that is catching on, but group performances. It is an updating of the London East End tradition of singing around a pub piano.

The first bar to introduce a karaoke night was Coates in the City. Others soon followed and it has now become part of pub culture, with most bars setting aside at least one night a week for karaoke. Many venues claim that even with the current recession, their takings double or even treble on karaoke night.

Turnmills, a restaurant in the City, started karaoke nights six months ago "They are very popular — extremely crowded. It's a fun night," says owner Jim Newman. With a night's gross sometimes up to 8,000 pounds (¥2 million), it is also highly profitable.

Turner. A full system is pricey, with a top-of-the-line set costing over 10,000 pounds (¥2.5 million).

Singing Machine has, however, just launched its own cheaper home karaoke set which plays ordinary audio tapes and can be plugged into a conventional stereo. At 325 pounds (¥81,000) it is for the enthusiast. The company hopes that as the awareness of karaoke grows, the home market will be as successful as it has been in pubs and clubs.

Many pubs in the UK now have karaoke nights, which are seen as big money-spinners. Some owners say that earnings treble on such nights.

Photo by Gareth Wyn Jones

IN BRIEF

JVC TO MARKET KARAOKE CD GRAPHICS UNITS

Victor Co of Japan (JVC) will next month begin marketing of compact disc graphics equipment designed specifically for karaoke, or sing-along systems. The company intends to export the systems to Taiwan later this year, and eventually to other Southeast Asian countries.

The CD graphics technology provides high quality sound

development of hardware and software for CD graphics systems with Daewoo Electronics Co., a major consumer electronics firm in South Korea.

(W, April 19, PR)

JAL PLANS TO LINK UP WITH DELTA AIRLINES

Japan Airlines Co. is aiming to link up with the U.S. carrier Delta Airlines by November to gain a foothold in the Caribbean travel market including

to Atlanta.

Sources said JAL aims to increase the number of its leisure travelers with connecting flights to Orlando, Florida; San Juan, Puerto Rico and Nassau in the former British territory of the Bahamas.

Delta and JAL will cooperate in seat sales on connecting flights by mutually reserving blocks of seats.

The two airlines also plan to work together to provide ground services, the sources said, including airport

The British press headlines the impact of *karaoke* in the UK,
11 May 1991.

associations with Japan. Others, as with the link between Komatsu City (Ishikawa) and Gateshead, have been based on recent Japanese investment in the UK or commercial ties.[18]

Reflection upon the Japanese influence on life in Europe would be incomplete without some mention of the impact of tourism. Figures have been previously given for the rising tide of Japanese short-term visitors passing in groups and even individually through the tourist capitals of Europe. Of the estimated 1.2 million who visited Europe in 1993, a total of 598,000 came to Britain.[19] The British Tourist Authority's 1991 campaign, 'Britain Welcomes the Japanese Visitor', paid heed to the importance and the spending power of these latter-day ambassadors from Japan. Another aspect of 'Japanization' surely lies in the response of hoteliers and businesspeople to the promise that this Japanese influx brings.

The Chairman of the Executive Committee of the British Tourist Authority's campaign, Countess Raine Spencer, stepmother of one of Britain's most prominent tourist attractions, the Princess of Wales, summed up some aspects of the changing Japanese face of Britain:

> Many hotels are taking infinite trouble, such as the Park Lane, which offers a Business Centre with Japanese translators, a free 'Asahi Shimbun', and menus and safety regulations in their own language . . . The Royal Crescent at Bath, and

In 1991 the British Tourist Authority launched its 'Britain Welcomes Japan' campaign (British Tourist Authority).

A Japanese promotion at Liberty's.

the George in Edinburgh employ Japanese nationals, as does the St Andrews Old Course Hotel, recognising the Japanese love of golf . . . The St James Court Hotel offers the Yellow Pages in Japanese to help their business visitors, apart from complimentary slippers and kimonos.[20]

London shops did not come out well from comparisons with Parisian boutiques, where service and packaging are much more to the Japanese taste. On the other hand, inroads have been made:

On the fashion front, Burberrys and Daks now make special clothes sizes for the Japanese and some shops do fast alterations . . . Harrods have inaugerated a Japanese Information desk at door 5, and are employing Japanese at their new store at Heathrow. Liberty's have a special training manual for their staff, and the Regent Street Association offers an elaborate guide to the Street in Japanese.[21]

Liberty's was at the forefront of nineteenth-century *japonisme* in Britain. Just as it then catered to the aesthetic taste of its Victorian customers, the Regent Street emporium today sells the 'Liberty Style' to a fashion-minded resident Japanese business community and to a tourist clientele. Between the two great waves of Japanization in Europe have come generations of diversity, assimilation and change.

6   Conclusion: Close Encounters of the Third Kind

For those familiar with cinema history and particularly the science fiction genre that deals with outer space, alien encounters, culture shock and survival of the fittest are not unfamiliar themes. Japan's relations with Europe, both past and present, have encompassed similar plots and have thrown up a host of exaggerated images and rhetoric which suggest that fantasy does not only confine itself to the celluloid sphere.

Trade and investment have been the platforms for the closest encounters between East and West. Japan's 'Christian Century' saw Japanese and Europeans coming face-to-face for the first time. The Dutch presence in Japan brought an awareness for some that the path to 'enlightenment' lay not only in the realm of indigenous beliefs. The reopening of Japan to trade in the 1850s set the agenda for future contact as, in Japan and Europe, competing commercial interests held sway. Japan's mirroring of the West in the Meiji period helped the country to industrialize and modernize at a remarkably rapid pace. That this process was undertaken with European and American support established bonds that have underpinned subsequent exchange.

But what of the comings and goings arising from such associations? The early Japanese missions to Europe and the European forays to Japan were eye-opening in their impact, while carving out images for the future to disinter. Individual travellers later expanded the compendium with more pointed insights borne of the experience of 'Europe' in all its separate parts and of the multiple faces of Japan.

In the postwar period, renewed contact with Europe through the resurgence of trade laid the groundwork for investment and an increased number of Japanese working and living abroad. American influence may have been dominant in Japan since the Occupation years but the third side of the 'skewed triangle' of Japan, US and European relations has gradually asserted itself. The 1985 Single European Act provided the spur for a great wave of Japanese foreign direct investment in the 1980s as the image of Europe as a battened-down 'Fortress' posed an unnerving threat to Japan's trading interests in the West.

If Japan and Europe became an 'item' with the approach of 1992, the completion of the Single European Market has turned an erstwhile series of encounters into a complex relationship of trade and investment links. The distance between these two furthest points of the triangle has narrowed as Japanese companies have established bases in Europe and Europeans have become more directly involved with Japan. Increased tourism from Japan has added to the intercourse through which Europe has become a more familiar place.

The influx of Japanese companies into Europe has brought new technology, training and management skills into the framework of western industrial practice along with a rigorous approach to quality control and increased productivity, derived from a culture in which manufacturing, as an occupation, is still accorded high status. While most major Japanese firms have made their investments in Europe in the run-up to 1992, the deepening of existing involvements and the enhancement of research and development capabilities would seem to hold out a beacon for future collaboration and exchange.

Not all such partnerships have gone without a hitch. Honda Motor Company's design-and-development collaboration with the Rover Group which began in 1979, foundered in 1994 when the German car giant BMW took over the majority shares in the British firm. Despite the severing of its financial links with Rover, the Japanese auto manufacturer chose to expand its production base in the UK rather than withdraw, demonstrating that Japan's relationship with Europe was not a hostage to individual corporate coups. Miyake Shojiro, President of Honda Motor Europe, put forward the Japanese position:

> Honda has had a long history in Europe and has established a very good relationship with European people and society. We have already established our own manufacturing facilities, and whichever way the commercial discussions with BMW go, nothing will affect our commitment to European and British industry. That commitment will not change.[1]

The interdependent perspective on the Japanese presence in Europe must nevertheless allow that the Japanese need to be there for access to domestic markets as well as acknowledging the contributions such investment has made to the economic regeneration of regions that have once known better times.

The impact of Japanese investment in Europe cannot, however, be measured in purely economic terms. For the Japanese company employee and his family, a posting to 'Delicious Britain', '*Romantische Deutschland*' or '*La Belle France*' may alter for ever fixed views of a continent that is more than the sum of its parts. There are those who continue to live *à la Japonaise* abroad and yet the growing awareness of different attitudes, lifestyles and approaches to work are contributing a foreign dimension to the forces of change in Japan. A *World Youth Survey* conducted in 1994 revealed that, given the choice, only 26 per cent of the young full-time Japanese workers polled would seek to remain working for the same company throughout their career.[2] Generational change and corporate restructurings are shifting the values and opportunities which once made lifetime employment a predictable and universally desirable goal.

A direct correlation between changing social values and exposure to different lifestyles overseas cannot readily be drawn. Out of a population of 124 million people, the numbers of Japanese who have accumulated such experience is necessarily small. Moves towards internationalization, however, have also brought increasing numbers of foreign students and workers into Japan. The unfavourable trade balance, meanwhile, is setting European governments' and companies' sights on foreign direct investment in Japan. As the encounters multiply, like the ripples made by pebbles in a pond, so too do the prospects for change.

For many Japanese who have faced the prospect of a posting in Europe, the expectations and the reality have proved to be dissimilar. The theme-park image so popular in Japan does not always gel with the practicalities of surviving on a different cultural 'planet'. The support and comfort offered up by transplanted aspects of home, from hairdressers to *sushi* bars, cannot offset the disorientation engendered by problems of communication, distance and separation from familiar Japanese groups.

Being in Europe does inevitably effect some change. Images are tempered by experience and long-held prejudices may evolve or erode. For some, the evolution is so complete that returning to Japan itself becomes a wrench in which a new and preferable lifestyle must be left behind. That this reverse culture shock is a recognized phenomenon is reflected in the open discussion in Japan of the 'returnee' syndrome.

For those Japanese children who have spent formative years of education in European local schools, memories of Europe do not easily fade. The younger generation may have once paid a price for Japan's corporate expansion overseas. Today the signs suggest that this new breed of

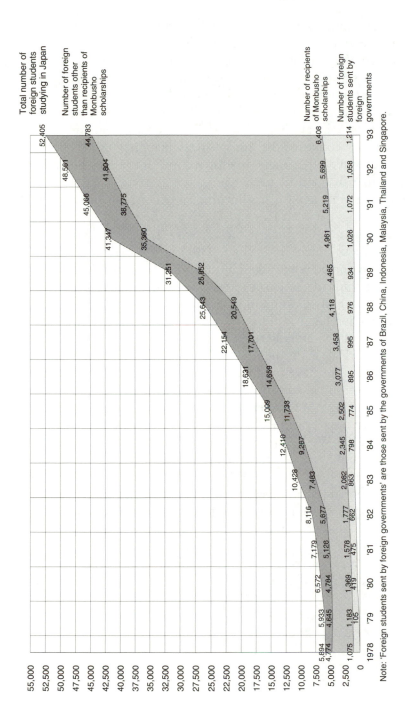

Graph showing trends in the numbers of foreign students in Japan (Monbusho).

Note: 'Foreign students sent by foreign governments' are those sent by the governments of Brazil, China, Indonesia, Malaysia, Thailand and Singapore.

'international youth' are forming an élite corps whose wider experience of the outside world will help to set the future course for Japan.

Encounters, of course, are never one-sided. The Japanese presence in Europe has made for contact and interaction that have broadened European perceptions of Japan and dulled the time-worn images of the past. Japanese people and culture – along with factories and cars – have come to Europe and have helped to redefine the European notion of Japan. If *japonisme* once conveyed the European fascination with Japan, the legacy of the recent wave of Japanese investment in Europe may be based more on social rather than artistic exchange.

The mixing of metaphors has become an occupational hazard for those charting meetings between East and West, yet the juxtaposition of cultural models and analogous forms has the capacity to yield the greater insights into common experience and values. The late historian of Japan, Richard Storry, once observed when asked by an audience of British schoolteachers to define the spirit of the Japanese tea ceremony, 'Well, it's pretty much a cross between Holy Communion and Cricket!' For the Japanese abroad seeking to comprehend some of the mysteries of European life, such an explanation could be usefully reversed.

From the arrival of Portuguese traders in sixteenth-century Japan, the Japanese and Europe have sought some common ground. First encounters were bound by mutual curiosity and interest with unfamiliarity giving rise to cultural exchange. Subsequent contact brought its share of mistrust and hostility, reaching a peak in the Second World War, as a Japan who so avidly copied the West soon outpaced its mentors. More recent history has seen Japan and Europe putting old quarrels to rest and re-entering, once again, the same sphere. This third encounter has been of a closer kind as business collaboration and investment have established firmer ties.

Lest old acquaintance be forgot, as the millennium approaches, various nations of Europe dwell on their initial meetings with Japan. The Dutch look forward to the year 2000 and marking the 400th anniversary of trade while Britain remembers that in 1600 William Adams became the first Englishman to arrive in Japan.

Notes

CHAPTER 1: JAPAN AND EUROPE

1   G.B.Sansom, *Japan: A Short Cultural History* (1962 edn), p.414.
2   Ibid., p.415.
3   G.B.Sansom, *The Western World and Japan* (1951 edn), p.115.
4   Donald F.Lach, *Japan in the Eyes of Europe* (1968 edn),p.664.
5   Ibid., p.670.
6   G.B.Sansom, *A History of Japan 1334–1615* (1961), pp.294–5.
7   Michael Sullivan, *The Meeting of Eastern and Western Art* (1973), pp.15–16.
8   Okamoto Yoshitomo, *The Namban Art of Japan* (1972), p.77.
9   J.F.Moran, *The Japanese and the Jesuits: Alessandro Valignano in Sixteenth-Century Japan* (1993), pp.8–9.
10 Ibid., p.11.
11 Ibid., p.10.
12 Lach, *Japan in the Eyes of Europe*, p.692.
13 Sansom, *The Western World and Japan* (1951), p.173.
14 Richard Storry, *A History of Modern Japan* (1961 edn), p.61.
15 Ibid., p.65.
16 Donald Keene, *The Japanese Discovery of Europe 1720–1830* (1969 edn), p.4.
17 Ibid., p.10.
18 Ibid., p.15.
19 Ibid., p.17.
20 G.B.Sansom, *A History of Japan 1615–1867* (1963 edn), p.189.
21 Keene, *The Japanese Discovery of Europe*, p.159.
22 Ibid., p.160.
23 Storry, *A History of Modern Japan*, p.66.
24 Hugh Cortazzi, *Victorians in Japan: In and Around the Treaty Ports* (1987), pp.xiv–xv.
25 H.J. Jones, *Live Machines: Hired Foreigners and Meiji Japan* (1980), p.xv and p.145.
26 D. Eleanor Westney, *Imitation and Innovation: The Transfer of Western Organizational Patterns to Meiji Japan* (1987), p.220.

27 Donald H. Shively, 'The Japanization of the Middle Meiji' in D. Shively (ed.) *Tradition and Modernization in Japanese Culture* (1971), p.94.

28 Kyooka Eiichi (tr.), *The Autobiography of Fukuzawa Yukichi* (1960 edn), pp.124–40.

29 Olive Checkland, *Britain's Encounter with Meiji Japan 1868–1912* (1989), p.139.

30 Ardath W.Burks (ed.), *The Modernizers: Overseas Students, Foreign Employees, and Meiji Japan* (1985), p.163.

31 Eugene Soviak, 'On the nature of western progress: the journal of the Iwakura embassy' in D. Shively (ed.) *Tradition and Modernization in Japanese Culture*, pp.15–16.

32 Ibid., p.17.

33 Ibid.

34 Ibid., P.19.

35 Hirakawa Sukehiro, 'Image of a British scholar – Natsume Soseki's reminiscences of his London days' in J.W.M. Chapman and J.P. Lehmann (eds) *Proceedings of the British Association for Japanese Studies*, vol.5, part 1 (1980), pp.168–70.

36 Helen Ballhatchet, 'Baba Tatsui (1850–1898) and Victorian Britain' in H. Cortazzi and G. Daniels (eds) *Britain and Japan 1859–1991: Themes and Personalities* (1991), p.111.

37 Sukehiro, op.cit., p.171.

38 Ibid., p.172.

39 Sir Rutherford Alcock, *Capital of the Tycoon* (1863) quoted in Jean-Pierre Lehmann, *The Image of Japan: From Feudal Isolation to World Power 1850–1905* (1978), pp.43–4.

40 Soviak, 'On the nature of western progress', p.12.

41 Pierre Loti, *Madame Chrysanthème* tr. L. Ensor (1987), p.73.

42 Edwin Arnold, *Seas and Lands* (1898) quoted in E. Wilkinson, *Japan Versus Europe: A History of Misunderstanding* (1983 edn), p.45.

43 Basil Hall Chamberlain, *Japanese Things* (1977 edn, previous editions entitled *Things Japanese*), p.3.

44 Ibid., p.7.

CHAPTER 2: THE ROAD TO 1992

1 W.G.Beasley, *The Modern History of Japan* (1981 edn), p.215.

2 Janet Hunter, *The Emergence of Modern Japan: An Introductory History from 1853* (1989), p.120.

3 Ibid., p.124.

4 Beasley, *The Modern History of Japan*.

5 Meirion and Susie Harries, *Sheathing the Sword: the Demilitarisation of Japan* (1987), p.20.

6 Hunter, *The Emergence of Modern Japan*, p.133.

7 Beasley, *The Modern History of Japan*, p.305.

8 E. Wilkinson, *Japan Versus Europe: A History of Misunderstanding* (1983 edn), p.169.

9 Roger Strange, *Japanese Manufacturing Investment in Europe: Its Impact on the UK Economy* (1993), p.85.

10 Ibid., p.86.

11 Ali M. El-Agraa, *Japan's Trade Frictions: Realities and Misconceptions* (1988), p.6.

12 Strange, *Japanese Manufacturing Investment in Europe*, p.89.

13 Wilkinson, *Japan versus Europe*, p.173.

14 Ibid.

15 Strange, *Japanese Manufacturing Investment in Europe*.

16 Ibid.

17 Wilkinson, *Japan versus Europe*, pp.189–90.

18 El-Agraa, *Japan's Trade Frictions*, p.5.

19 Strange, *Japanese Manufacturing Investment in Europe*, p.91.

20 Ishikawa Kaoru, 'Relations with Europe: handle with care', *Japan Echo*, 18, 4 (Winter 1991), p.71.

21 El Agraa, *Japan's Trade Frictions*, p.6.

22 Peter Dicken, 'The changing geography of Japanese foreign direct investment in manufacturing industry: a global perspective' in Jonathon Morris (ed.), *Japan and the Global Economy: Issues and Trends in the 1990s* (1991). For a general discussion of the early history of FDI, see ibid., pp.25–9.

23 Akimune Ichiro, 'Overview: Japan's direct investment in the EC' in M. Yoshitomi *et al.*, *Japanese Direct Investment in Europe: Motives, Impact and Policy Implications*, vol.II (1990), p.8.

24 Dicken, 'The changing geography of Japanese foreign direct investment', p.29.

25 Ibid.

26 Ibid., p.36–7.

27 Strange, op.cit., p.52.

28 Statistics from JETRO and Jonathan Morris, 'Japanese manufacturing investment in the EC: an overview' in J. Morris (ed.) *Japan and the Global Economy: Issues and Trends in the 1990s* (1991), p.196.

29 Statistics from JETRO and Ministry of Finance (1993).

30 Brian Bridges, *EC–Japan Relations: In Search of a Partnership* (1992), p.5, and Ministry of Finance statistics.

31 Akimune, 'Overview: Japan's direct investment in the EC', p.15.

32 All statistics from JETRO and Ministry of Finance (1993).

33 Morris, 'Japanese manufacturing investment in the EC', p.199.

34 Strange, *Japanese Manufacturing Investment in Europe*, p.100.

35 'Japanese views of Europe', *Japan Echo*, 19, 3 (Autumn 1992), p.59.

36 Strange, *Japanese Manufacturing Investment in Europe*, pp.85-86.

37 Kitamura Hiroshi, 'The subtlety and tenacity of British diplomacy: lessons for Japan' in *Japan Echo*, 19, 3 (Autumn 1992), pp.63–4.

38 Based on trade figures for 1993 as supplied by JETRO.

39 Ibid.

40 Wilkinson, *Japan Versus Europe*, pp.203–4.

41 Ishikawa, 'Relations with Europe', p.74.

42 'Japan protests over Cresson's attack on trade', *Financial Times*, 30 May 1991, p.1.

43 Ishikawa, 'Relations with Europe', p.72.

44 'Friendship of the cut-throat kind', *The Times*, 22 May 1991, p.14.

45 Ishikawa, 'Relations with Europe'.

46 'The Japanese Government's basic policy towards the EC' in Bridges, *EC–Japan Relations*, Appendix 3, p.38.

47 'Joint Declaration on relations between the EC and its member states and Japan, July 1991' in Bridges, *EC–Japan Relations*, Appendix 1, pp.28–30.
48 *Overview of EC Japan Relations*, EC Commission Report, 24 January 1994, pp.1–2.
49 Ibid., p.9.
50 Jean-Pierre Leng, 'Europe and Japan: forging closer links', in *Journal of Japanese Trade and Industry*, 4 (1992), p.45.
51 'Japan–European Community economic relations: a proposal for tomorrow', *Anglo Japanese Journal*, 6, 3 (January–March 1993), p.8.
52 'Strengthen ties with EC now, panel urges', *Nikkei Weekly*, 21 December 1992, p.3.
53 Douglas Hurd, 'The 1990s: challenges for trade', *Anglo Japanese Journal*, 4, 1 (April–June 1990), p.5.

CHAPTER 3: LIVING IN EUROPE

1 As the Japanese business community in Europe consists mainly of male company employees, most references in the text that follows are to Japanese businessmen.
 2 Statistics supplied by Asia Department, British Tourist Authority, London, 1994.
 3 Okakura Tenshin quoted in E. Wilkinson, *Japan Versus Europe* (1983), p.115.
 4 Alan Takeo Moriyama, *Imingaisha* (1985), p.xvii.
 5 Statistics supplied by Japan National Tourist Organization and Asia Department, British Tourist Authority, London,1994.
 6 *Japan: ABTA Market Guide* (1991), p.21.
 7 James Clavell, *Gai-jin* (1993).
 8 Nakane Chie, *Japanese Society* (1970), pp.130–1.
 9 Joy Hendry, *Understanding Japanese Society* (1987), p.49.
10 Merry White, *The Japanese Overseas: Can They Go Home Again?* (1988), p.82.
11 Ezra Vogel, *Japan As No. 1: Lessons for America* (1985 edn), p.148.
12 Nakane, *Japanese Society*, p.136.
13 Robert M. March, *Working for a Japanese Company: Insights Into the Multicultural Workplace* (1992). p.40.
14 Peter Dale, *The Myth of Japanese Uniqueness* (1986), introduction.
15 Interview, Hagiwara Atsushi, President, Nissan Motor Deutschland GMBH, Düsseldorf, May 1992.
16 March, *Working for a Japanese Company*, p.41.
17 Ronald Dore and Mari Sako, *How the Japanese Learn to Work* (1989), p.11.
18 Ibid., p.5.
19 JET statistics from Council for Local Authorities for International Relations quoted in *The Japan Times*, 25 July 1994, p.8.
20 White, *The Japanese Overseas*, p.46.
21 All statistics as published by Monbusho. Eleven of the 32 full-time Japanese schools in Europe are privately run.
22 For a full treatment of the subject, see Roger Goodman, *Japan's International Youth: The Emergence of a New Class of Schoolchildren* (1993 edn).
23 Ibid., p.5.

24 White, *The Japanese Overseas*, pp.76–9.

CHAPTER 4: THE JAPANESE IN EUROPE

 1 Oba Sadao, 'The Japanese community in Britain 1870–1945', Lecture delivered
    to the Japan Society,14 September 1993.
 2 Ibid.
 3 Kitamura Toshiharu, 'Investment in financial services' in Sumitomo Life
    Research Institute, *Japanese Direct Investment in Europe* (1990), p.108.
 4 Statistics from Embassy of Japan, London. Text reproduced in part from
    paper prepared for the UK-Japan 2000 Group on 'Japanese residents in the
    UK' (1993).
 5 Kitamura Hiroshi, *Japan and Britain: The Global Context of a Dynamic Partnership*
    (1993), p.18.
 6 Ibid., p.19.
 7 Statistics from JETRO, *The Survey of European Operations of Japanese Companies
    in the Manufacturing Sector* (1993), pp.2,4,5, and 10.
 8 David Bowen, 'Made in Japan, sold on Britain' in *The Independent on Sunday*, 15
    August 1993, p.14.
 9 James Daniel, 'Writer reveals the rich layers of UK culture' in *The Japan Times*,
    2 February 1992, p.9.
10 Osamu Nawa, 'Anglophile sees British boom' in *Nikkei Weekly*, 19 April
    1993, p.20.
11 J. Morris, M. Munday and B. Wilkinson, *Working for the Japanese: The Economic
    and Social Consequences of Japanese Investment in Wales* (1993), p.123.
12 'Japon Économie et Société', no.259, 1 October 1993, p.12.
13 Interview with Kawahara Tatsu, Vice President, Mitsui & Co. France SA, Paris,
    16 February 1994.
14 Interview with Abe Yoshio, Secretary General, Japanese Chamber of Commerce
    and Industry in France, Paris, 16 February 1994.
15 JETRO, *The Survey of European Operations of Japanese Companies*, p.4.
16 Graham Lord, 'Why the French are flirting with Japan' in *Insight Japan*, February
    1993, 1, 3, p.5.
17 Statistics provided by the Embassy of Japan, Paris, February 1994. Of the
    total 18,289 Japanese residents registered, the breakdown according to type is
    as follows:

Business residents (including families)	7157
Journalists	214
Artists and other unaffiliated groups	1352
Students, teachers and researchers	4777
Government officials	1017
Others	1219
Permanent residents	2553

18 Interview with Hasegawa Michio, President/Director General, Saint-Germain
    France SA, Paris, 15 February 1994.
19 Interview with Koito Junji, Secretariat, Association Amicale des Ressortissants
    Japonais en France (Nihonjinkai), Paris, 16 February 1994.
20 Others include: *OVNI, Paris Dayori, K.S.M.Shukan Scraps, France News Digest*
    and *Nikkan Media Digest*.

21   Interview with Professor Muta Yasuaki, L'Institut Culturel Franco Japonais, Montigny-le-Bretonneux, 15 February 1994.
22   Ibid.
23   Quoted in Kimura Hiroko, 'Japan's world view praised', *The Japan Times*, 14 July 1993, p.6.
24   Dr Ota Hiroaki, *Le Syndrome de Paris* (1991).
25   Imakita Junichi, 'Relations begin person-to-person' in *The Japan Times*, 14 July 1994, p.15.
26   Chairman, Sony France, 'The enterprise culture of the Sony Group', October 1992.
27   Nakamura Yoko, 'Japan's images of Germany change with passing of time', *The Japan Times*, 27 February 1993, B5.
28   Mukata Ryohei, 'Bringing Europe and Japan closer together: how to reap a bountiful harvest' in *Euro Japanese Journal*, 1, 1 (April–July 1994), p.3.
29   Quoted in Nakamura, 'Japan's images of Germany'.
30   Ibid.
31   Ibid.
32   F.N. Burton and S.F. Saelen, 'The Structure and Characteristics of Japanese Foreign Direct Investment in West Germany' in *Management Today*, 20, 4 (1980), p.10.
33   Kitamura Toshiharu, 'Investment in financial services', p.111.
34   Kume G. and Totsuka K., 'Japanese Manufacturing Investment in the EC: Motives and Locations' in Sumitomo Life Research Institute, *Japanese Direct Investment in Europe* (1990), pp.46–7.
35   Interview with Wolfgang Jansen, NRW Economic Development Corporation, Düsseldorf, 20 May 1992.
36   Statistics from JETRO, *The Survey of European Operations of Japanese Companies*.
37   Ibid.
38   Interview with Matsuda Toshifumi, Principal, *Japanische Internationale Schüle*, Düsseldorf, 21 May 1992.
39   Interview with Inoue Toshihiro, Nagasaki Holland Village Nederland, The Hague, 27 April 1994.
40   Statistics from the Netherlands Foreign Investment Agency (1993).
41   Ibid.
42   Statistics from Embassy of Japan, The Hague (1994).
43   Statistics from JETRO, *The Survey of European Operations of Japanese Companies*.
44   Statistics from Embassy of Japan, The Hague, (1994).
45   Interview with Mrs Osada, JCCI, Amsterdam, 25 April 1994.
46   Interview with Maiya Masahiko, President and Managing Director, Hotel Okura, Amsterdam, 25 April 1994.
47   Statistics from JETRO, *The Survey of European Operations of Japanese Companies*.
48   Harashima Masae, quoted in 'Japanese firms impact European industrial culture', *Nikkei Weekly*, 13 June 1992, p.18.
49   Interview with Sakaguchi Toshihiko, Commercial Attaché, Embassy of Japan, Brussels, 21 January 1994.
50   Ibid.
51   Interview with Sato Masahiko and Miyasako Matsuo, Chairman and Secretary General, Nihonjinkai, Brussels, 21 January 1994.

52 Eugene Soviak, 'On the nature of western progress: the journal of the Iwakura Embassy' in D. Shiveley (ed.), *Tradition and Modernization in Japanese Culture* (1971), p.16.

53 Ibid., p.29.

54 Statistics from Embassy of Japan, Madrid (1994).

55 John Parry, 'Japan in Europe: The Spanish Experience' in *Anglo Japanese Journal*, 6, 1 (May–August 1992), p.17.

56 Statistics from JETRO, Madrid (1994).

57 Ibid.

58 Nozawa Koji, 'Japanese investors believe in Catalonia's economic potential' in *Nikkei Weekly*, 11 July 1994, p.5.

59 Statistics from JETRO, Madrid (1994).

60 Statistics from Embassy of Japan, Madrid and Consulate General, Barcelona (1994).

61 Interview with Suzuki Toshiyuki, Japanese Consul, Barcelona, 9 May 1994.

62 Interview with Nemoto Eri, CIDEM, Barcelona, 9 May 1994.

63 Janina M.de Guzman, 'Don Quixote dreamland hovers on Mie shores' in *Japan Times*, 3 July 1994, p.12.

CHAPTER 5: THE JAPANIZATION OF EUROPE

1 Nick Oliver and Barry Wilkinson, *The Japanization of British Industry* (1992), p.1.

2 Max Munday, *Japanese Manufacturing Investment in Wales* (1990), p.132.

3 Ibid.

4 Sue Milsome, *The Impact of Japanese Firms on Working and Employment Practices in British Manufacturing Industry*, a review of recent research conducted on behalf of the Department of Employment, March 1993, p.108.

5 Ibid., p.110.

6 Oliver and Wilkinson, *The Japanization of British Industry*, p.164.

7 Jean-Pierre Lehmann, 'France, Japan, Europe, and industrial competition: the automotive case', *International Affairs*, 68, 1 (January 1992), p.44.

8 Nicholas Wolfers, foreword, *The Great Japan Exhibition* (1981), p.15.

9 Sir Peter Parker quoted in 'UK–Japan educational and cultural exchange' (draft), RIIA and Japan Center for Educational Exchange (1993), p.32.

10 *Guide to the Japan Pavilion* , Expo'92, p.16.

11 Kaifu Toshiki quoted in *EC-Japan Fest, 'Antwerpen '93' Report*, 25 October 1993.

12 Takeuchi Haruhisa, 'Letter from JICC . . .', *Japan*, 575 (6 September 1994).

13 'Daiwa Foundation Japan House Opens' in *Japan*, 574 (2 August 1994) and *UK–Japan Relations – We Look Ahead*, Note by UK–Japan 2000 Group.

14 Statistics provided by Embassy of Japan, Paris (1994).

15 Murata Ryohei, 'Bringing Europe and Japan together: how to reap a bountiful harvest' in *Euro Japanese Journal*, 1, 1 (April–July 1994), p.3.

16 UK–Japan 2000 Group, 'Japanese language teaching at British universities and centres of higher education, a survey', December 1993.

17 Adriano Boscaro et al. (eds), *20th Anniversary EAJS: Past, Present and Future of the EAJS 1973–94* (1994), p.7. In addition to the British Association for Japanese Studies in the UK, the following Japanese studies associations are in operation in

Europe: The Austrian Association for Japanese Studies (Akademisher Arbeitskreis Japan); The French Society for Japanese Studies (Société Francaise des Études Japonaises); The German Association for Japanese Studies (Gesellschaft fur Japanforschung); The Italian Association for Japanese Studies (Associazione Italiana per gli Studi Giapponesi); The Netherlands Association for Japanese Studies (Het Nederlands Genootschap voor Japanse Studien); The Nordic Association for Japanese and Korean Studies.

18   Other twinning ties exist between: Strathkelvin (Scotland) and Yoichi (Hokkaido); Ottery St.Mary (Devon) and Otari-cho (Nagano); Alyn and Deeside (Wales) and Murato-cho (Miyagi).

19   Figures from Asia Department, British Tourist Authority, London (1994).

20   British Tourist Authority, *Britain Welcomes Japan: Caring for the Japanese Visitor* (1991), pp.6–7.

21   Ibid.

CHAPTER 6: CONCLUSION

1   Miyake Shojiro, quoted in 'Honda to carry on in UK', *Japan Contact*, 27 (April 1994).

2   Data taken from *World Youth Survey* (1994) conducted by the Youth Affairs Administration Bureau of the Management and Coordination Agency.

Select Bibliography

Beasley, W.G., *The Modern History of Japan* (1981 edn).

Checkland, Olive, *Britain's Encounter with Meiji Japan 1868–1912* (1989).

Conte-Helm, Marie, *Japan and the North East of England: From 1862 to the Present Day* (1989).

Dore, Ronald and Sako, Mari, *How the Japanese Learn to Work* (1989).

Dunning, John H., *Japanese Participation in British Industry* (1986).

El-Agraa, Ali M., *Japan's Trade Frictions: Realities and Misconceptions* (1988).

Goodman, Roger, *Japan's International Youth: The Emergence of a New Class of Schoolchildren* (1993 edn).

Japan Festival 1991 Archive Material (Victoria & Albert Museum).

Japan Foundation, 'Overview of Programmes' and 'Annual Reports'.

Jones, Stephanie, *Working for the Japanese: Myths and Realities – British Perceptions* (1991).

Keene, Donald, *The Japanese Discovery of Europe 1720–1830* (1969 edn).

Lehmann, Jean-Pierre, *The Image of Japan: From Feudal Isolation to World Power 1850–1905* (1978).

Morris, Jonathan (ed.), *Japan and the Global Economy: Issues and Trends in the 1990s* (1991).

Morris, J., Munday, M., Wilkinson, B., *Working for the Japanese: The Economic and Social Consequences of Japanese Investment in Wales* (1993).

Munday, Max, *Japanese Manufacturing Investment in Wales* (1990).

Oliver, Nick and Wilkinson, Barry, *The Japanization of British Industry: New Developments in the 1990s* (1992).

Royal Institute of International Affairs and Japan Center for International Exchange (eds), *Britain and Japan: the New Era. A Review of UK–Japan Bilateral Activities* (1994).

Sansom, G.B., *The Western World and Japan* (1951 edn).

Strange, Roger, *Japanese Manufacturing Investment in Europe: Its Impact on the UK Economy* (1993).

White, Merry, *The Japanese Overseas: Can They Go Home Again?* (1988).

White, Michael and Trevor, Malcolm, *Under Japanese Management: The Experience of British Workers* (1983).

Wilkinson, Endymion, *Japan Versus Europe: A History of Misunderstanding* (1983).

Yoshitomi, Masaru (ed.), *Japanese Direct Investment in Europe: Motives, Impact and Policy Implications*, Vol.II, (1990).

Index